SpringerBriefs in Law

SpringerBriefs present concise summaries of cutting-edge research and practical applications across a wide spectrum of fields. Featuring compact volumes of 50 to 125 pages, the series covers a range of content from professional to academic. Typical topics might include:

- A timely report of state-of-the art analytical techniques
- A bridge between new research results, as published in journal articles, and a contextual literature review
- A snapshot of a hot or emerging topic
- A presentation of core concepts that students must understand in order to make independent contributions

SpringerBriefs in Law showcase emerging theory, empirical research, and practical application in Law from a global author community. SpringerBriefs are characterized by fast, global electronic dissemination, standard publishing contracts, standardized manuscript preparation and formatting guidelines, and expedited production schedules.

Svitlana Mazepa

War, Hate, Propaganda and the Internet: A Dangerous Combination

Svitlana Mazepa ⓘ
University of Osnabrück
Osnabrück, Germany

Department of Criminal Law and Procedure
West Ukrainian National University
Ternopil, Ukraine

ISSN 2192-855X   ISSN 2192-8568 (electronic)
SpringerBriefs in Law
ISBN 978-3-031-69007-5   ISBN 978-3-031-69008-2 (eBook)
https://doi.org/10.1007/978-3-031-69008-2

This research was funded by the VolkswagenStiftung (Volkswagen Foundation) under the framework of the Visiting Research Programme for Ukrainian academics fleeing the war.

© The Author(s), under exclusive license to Springer Nature Switzerland AG 2024

This work is subject to copyright. All rights are solely and exclusively licensed by the Publisher, whether the whole or part of the material is concerned, specifically the rights of translation, reprinting, reuse of illustrations, recitation, broadcasting, reproduction on microfilms or in any other physical way, and transmission or information storage and retrieval, electronic adaptation, computer software, or by similar or dissimilar methodology now known or hereafter developed.
The use of general descriptive names, registered names, trademarks, service marks, etc. in this publication does not imply, even in the absence of a specific statement, that such names are exempt from the relevant protective laws and regulations and therefore free for general use.
The publisher, the authors and the editors are safe to assume that the advice and information in this book are believed to be true and accurate at the date of publication. Neither the publisher nor the authors or the editors give a warranty, expressed or implied, with respect to the material contained herein or for any errors or omissions that may have been made. The publisher remains neutral with regard to jurisdictional claims in published maps and institutional affiliations.

This Springer imprint is published by the registered company Springer Nature Switzerland AG
The registered company address is: Gewerbestrasse 11, 6330 Cham, Switzerland

If disposing of this product, please recycle the paper.

Acknowledgements

I would like to thank Osnabrueck University and the Centre for European and International Criminal Law Studies for the opportunity to work in a wonderful, friendly atmosphere using valuable contacts and resources. I am also grateful to my host professor Prof. Dr. Arndt Sinn, who supported me all the time I was working on the manuscript.

Contents

1 **Introduction** 1
  References 5
2 **Diagnostics of Destructive Propaganda** 7
  References 9
3 **Ukraine's Reaction to Propaganda in Wartime Conditions** 11
  References 13
4 **Ukrainian Cases on the Propaganda of Changing
  the Constitutional Order or State Borders** 15
  4.1 Court Judgments Declaring Propaganda Content as Criminal 16
  4.2 Court Verdicts Where the Dissemination of Propaganda Content
      Was Justified 18
  4.3 Court Verdicts Against People Who Spread Communist Symbols ... 23
  References 24
5 **Hate Speech** 27
  5.1 Some Ukrainian Cases Involving Hate Speech 31
  5.2 Some German Cases About Hate Speech 35
  5.3 NetzDG 36
  References 37
6 **Freedom of Speech in the Conditions of an Armed Conflict** 41
  6.1 Searching for a Balance Between Criticism of the Government
      in Wartime, a Refusal to Mobilise and the Protection of National
      Interests on the Example of Ukraine 43
  6.2 The Issue of Ethnic Relations and Hate Speech Using
      the Example of Bosnia 44

    6.3   The Duty of the Press to Share Information and Ideas on Policy Issues, Including Controversial Ones, and the Public's Right to Receive Them—Using the Example of Turkey 47
References 48
7 Conclusion 49
References 51

Chapter 1
Introduction

War is always a direct attack on the rule of law and most important human rights and freedoms. It is why the United Nations organisation was established after World War Two, with its main goal being to maintain international peace and security. Under the UN Charter and the Rome Statute of the International Criminal Court, the crime of aggression is considered the most serious violation. However, in today's conflicts, particular attention should be paid to the information war that, using the tools of propaganda, disinformation and fakes, is aimed at manipulating the consciousness of society worldwide, fomenting enmity and inciting others to commit crimes.[1]

The full-scale invasion of the Russian Federation of Ukraine has now been going on for more than two years and there is little doubt that it constitutes the first real cyberwar our world has experienced. The Russian Federation is spending vast sums on spreading propaganda and disinformation among the population through information devices using modern technologies. The first thing the Russian military did when they intervened in the Ukrainian state was to cut off the technical access of Ukrainian citizens to sources of information as much as possible, leaving people unable to find out the real picture of events. A lot of special equipment was imported that broadcast fakes and Russian propaganda. Proof of this is a report about a crucified boy, a news story that flew all over the world and was later retracted as false.[2]

Information security of Ukraine is an integral part of the national security of Ukraine. This means a level of protection of state sovereignty, territorial integrity, democratic constitutional order and other vital interests of man, society and the state in which the constitutional rights and freedoms are properly ensured. It also involves ensuring access to reliable and objective information and the country has in place an effective system of protection and countermeasures against harm caused by the spread of negative informational influences, including the coordinated spread of unreliable

---

[1] Mazepa (2024). Some research results were published in the mentioned article in Ukrainian.
[2] Official website of National Ukrainian TV channel : https://tsn.ua/video/video-novini/rosiyske-tb-viznalo-scho-rozp-yatiy-hlopchik-buv-feykom.html. Accessed 15 April 2024.

information, destructive propaganda, other information operations.[3] Therefore, countering the spread of propaganda is considered a component of ensuring the country's information security.

Russian propaganda can also exacerbate underlying social and political tensions by promoting divisive or extremist views. By exploiting existing fractures in society, propaganda can intensify existing conflicts and make their resolution more difficult. This can create a more polarised and volatile political environment.

In addition, Russian propaganda can be used to undermine the credibility and legitimacy of other countries and their leaders. By spreading false or misleading information about other countries, Russia can weaken their international position and gain a strategic advantage.

Overall, the dangers of Russian propaganda are significant and it is important for people to be aware of these risks in order to take steps to counter them. This could include increasing media literacy, supporting independent journalism and developing effective strategies to counter disinformation.

Numerous studies and reports have been conducted on the impact of Russian propaganda, and the results vary depending on the specific context and methods of analysis. Here are some examples of statistics related to the influence of Russian propaganda:

According to a 2018 Pew Research Center study, 72% of Americans believed that Russia's efforts to interfere in the 2016 US presidential election were at least somewhat successful. This suggests that Russian propaganda and disinformation campaigns may have had some effect on public opinion in the US.[4]

In a 2018 survey of residents of seven European countries by the EU's External Action Service, 59% of respondents said they were aware of Russian propaganda, while 44% said they had seen examples of it. However, only 16% of respondents said they believed that Russian propaganda had influenced their personal opinion.[5]

A study by the Oxford Internet Institute found that Russian propaganda and disinformation campaigns were particularly effective at spreading false information on social media during the 2016 US presidential election. A study found that 4% of Twitter users exposed to Russian propaganda during the election subsequently retweeted it.[6]

Another study by researchers at the University of Pennsylvania found that Russian propaganda on Facebook and Instagram during the 2016 US election may have

---

[3] The information security strategy was approved by Presidential Decree No. 685/2021 of 28 December 2021.
https://zakon.rada.gov.ua/laws/show/685/2021#Text. Accessed 15 April 2024.

[4] Pew Research Center study on Americans' views of Russian election interference: https://www.pewresearch.org/politics/2018/03/01/americans-views-of-russia-and-russian-people-turn-sharply-negative/. Accessed 20 April 2024.

[5] European Union External Action Service survey on awareness of Russian propaganda in Europe: https://eeas.europa.eu/headquarters/headquarters-homepage/41001/public-opinion-poll-examines-awareness-and-perception-russian-disinformation-european-union_en. Accessed 22 April 2024.

[6] Oxford Internet Institute study on the spread of Russian propaganda on Twitter: https://www.oii.ox.ac.uk/blog/russian-trolls-are-the-15ers-who-helped-trump-win/. Accessed 22 April 2024.

reached 126 million Americans. The study also found evidence that the propaganda may have been particularly effective against conservative voters.[7]

The impact of Russian propaganda on the conflict in eastern Ukraine is a complex and controversial topic, and it is difficult to quantify the precise impact of propaganda on public opinion and political outcomes. However, here are some statistics related to this issue:

According to a 2019 survey conducted by the International Republican Institute, 37% of respondents in the Donetsk and Luhansk regions of Ukraine believe that the Ukrainian government is responsible for the conflict, while only 6% believe that Russia is responsible. This shows that Russian propaganda could have been successful in shaping the perception of the conflict in eastern Ukraine.[8]

A 2018 report by the NATO Strategic Communications Centre of Excellence analysed Russian propaganda efforts in Ukraine from 2014 to 2018 and found that the Russian media were able to reach a significant audience in eastern Ukraine. The report notes that Russian propaganda has been particularly effective in spreading conspiracy theories and discrediting the Ukrainian government.[9]

It is important to note that such statistics provide a limited understanding of the impact of Russian propaganda, with an ongoing debate among researchers and policymakers about the true extent of its influence.

Article 19 of the United Nation Universal Declaration of Human Rights states that everyone has the right to freedom of belief and expression. This provision is reflected in the national legislation of various countries, which also covers permitted censorship or restrictions on expressing certain opinions, including hate speech.[10] There are two diametrically different approaches to this issue. The first demonstrates the advantage of being open to a diversity of ideas where there are no limits on self-expression. The best response to hurtful speech is a discussion that allows different ideas to be freely expressed. Another approach is to limit hate speech, which is vital to the protection of minority communities from the harm that such speech causes. Different approaches to what constitutes acceptable speech can be seen around the world. The United States of America has traditionally been a country where constitutional protections for free speech have been staunchly defended.[11] However, even there are many restrictions on free speech, such as the banning of words that incite

---

[7] University of Pennsylvania study on the reach of Russian propaganda on Facebook and Instagram: https://www.nytimes.com/2017/10/30/technology/facebook-google-russian-ads.html. Accessed 20 April 2024.

[8] International Republican Institute survey on perceptions of the conflict in eastern Ukraine: https://www.iri.org/sites/default/files/iri_donetsk_luhansk_survey_december_2019.pdf. Accessed 25 April 2024.

[9] NATO Strategic Communications Centre of Excellence report on Russian propaganda in Ukraine: https://www.stratcomcoe.org/analysis-russian-propaganda-war-ukraine-2014-2018. Accessed 25 April 2024.

[10] Universal Declaration of Human Rights https://www.un.org/en/about-us/universal-declaration-of-human-rights. Accessed 25 April 2024.

[11] Fisch (2002).

"imminent unlawful acts" and those that "censor obscenity." Some European countries, in accordance with a decision of the Council of the European Union, have made it an offence not only for inciting hatred, but also for publicly denying crimes of genocide (for example, the Holocaust) or war crimes. In some Islamic countries, severe restrictions on freedom of speech can lead to the death penalty for such crimes[12] as apostasy, blasphemy or other actions against religion.[13] Furthermore, in Canada, for example, various laws at the federal, provincial and territorial levels impose restrictions on freedom of expression in the form of criminal prohibitions on defamation, fraud, etc.[14]

In Ukraine, the principle of freedom of speech is enshrined in Article 34 of the Constitution of Ukraine.[15] The concept of "freedom of speech" is quite broad and requires certain restrictions to prevent discrimination. How can one find a balance between propaganda and freedom of speech? An answer can be found thanks to an analysis of the European Court of Human Rights case law.

Freedom of speech is a fundamental right in a democratic society and is the basis for every person's development. In the course of the judicial practice of the European Court of Human Rights, criteria were developed for determining the correctness and expediency of restrictions on freedom of speech. This is necessary in a democratic society, which is provided for by law and is proportionate to the legitimate goal being pursued. Therefore, the state's restriction of freedom of speech is justified if it is carried out on the basis of morality, taking into account specified criteria. At the same time, legislation may limit the freedom of speech in some cases that concern very important spheres of societal life, provided that such a restriction can benefit society as a whole. Therefore, citizens should be certain that any violated right must be protected and restored, as there are legal grounds for doing so.

This book is intended to reveal the following key questions:

- Does the armed conflict change the limits on the freedom of speech, and what happens to this fundamental right after the war?
- What interference with freedom of speech does the European Court of Human Rights allow in the context of armed conflicts?

An analysis of judicial practice shows that the presence of evaluative judgments in criminal cases is a real challenge for judges and doubts about the interpretation of the content should be considered in favour of the accused.

---

[12] Adil (2007).

[13] Saeed (2017).

[14] Walker (2018).

[15] Constitution of Ukraine (1996). https://zakon.rada.gov.ua/laws/show/254%D0%BA/96-%D0%B2%D1%80#Text. Accessed 25 Apr 2024.

References

Adil MAM (2007) Law of apostasy and freedom of religion in Malaysia. Asian J Comparative Law 2:1–36

Constitution of Ukraine (1996). https://zakon.rada.gov.ua/laws/show/254%D0%BA/96-%D0%B2%D1%80#Text. Accessed 25 Apr 2024

European Union External Action Service survey on awareness of Russian propaganda in Europe. https://eeas.europa.eu/headquarters/headquarters-homepage/41001/public-opinion-poll-examines-awareness-and-perception-russian-disinformation-european-union_en. Accessed 22 Apr 2024

Fisch WB (2002) Hate speech in the constitutional law of the United States. Am J Comparative Law 50:463

International Republican Institute survey on perceptions of the conflict in eastern Ukraine. https://www.iri.org/sites/default/files/iri_donetsk_luhansk_survey_december_2019.pdf. Accessed 25 Apr 2024

Mazepa S (2024) A dangerous combination of the propaganda and the internet in the conditions of the Russian–Ukrainian war. Law of Ukraine. No. 1

NATO Strategic Communications Centre of Excellence report on Russian propaganda in Ukraine. https://www.stratcomcoe.org/analysis-russian-propaganda-war-ukraine-2014-2018. Accessed 25 Apr 2024

Official website of National Ukrainian TV channel. https://tsn.ua/video/video-novini/rosiyske-tb-viznalo-scho-rozp-yatiy-hlopchik-buv-feykom.html. Accessed 15 Apr 2024

Oxford Internet Institute study on the spread of Russian propaganda on Twitter. https://www.oii.ox.ac.uk/blog/russian-trolls-are-the-15ers-who-helped-trump-win/. Accessed 22 Apr 2024

Pew Research Center study on Americans' views of Russian election interference. https://www.pewresearch.org/politics/2018/03/01/americans-views-of-russia-and-russian-people-turn-sharply-negative/. Accessed 20 Apr 2024

Saeed A (2017) Freedom of religion, apostasy and Islam. Routledge

The information security strategy has been approved by Presidential Decree No. 685/2021 of 28 December 2021. https://zakon.rada.gov.ua/laws/show/685/2021#Text. Accessed 15 Apr 2024

Universal Declaration of Human Rights. https://www.un.org/en/about-us/universal-declaration-of-human-rights. Accessed 25 Apr 2024

University of Pennsylvania study on the reach of Russian propaganda on Facebook and Instagram. https://www.nytimes.com/2017/10/30/technology/facebook-google-russian-ads.html. Accessed 20 Apr 2024

Walker J (2018) Hate speech and freedom of expression: legal boundaries in Canada

Chapter 2
Diagnostics of Destructive Propaganda

To provide recommendations on ensuring the information security of the state as a whole and countering destructive propaganda, hate speech and the manipulation of human consciousness, it is necessary to look at the root of the problem. Applying the approach of medical diagnosis in the field of internet regulation is a new method of identifying problems. The most important thing is to adapt the methods of comparative law to formulate a more flexible framework that will reveal the reality of today's digital media problems. Given the unique institutional and media experience, the harmonisation of normative legal acts through legal translation should be rejected. It may be subject to manipulation by non-democratic states to establish state propaganda and censorship on the internet. In addition, the idea of internationally recognised hate speech that applies to all jurisdictions is debatable. New disciplines such as media ecology and media literacy are helping to unravel the links between hate speech and online violence. This facilitates the study of symptoms and root causes, thereby improving the effectiveness of diagnosis and response. First, it is necessary to study and evaluate the media environment for identifying social diseases that need "treatment." A flexible approach to mass media regulation should include equality and a respect for diversity, tolerance and pluralism. These components can only take place as a result of a preliminary study of the experience of scientific predecessors.[1]

In its cases, the European Court of Human Rights determines the legality, legitimacy and proportionality of restrictions on freedom of expression and "balances"[2] freedom of expression with conflicting rights and interests on an ad hoc basis.

Cases concerning matters of public interest for a democratic society deserve special attention. There is no clear definition of "public interest" in the case law of the European Court of Human Rights, but the case law contains a wide range of precedents that relate to various spheres of public life. It is certainly imperative to examine the diverse responses to disinformation around the world and to develop a

---

[1] Rinceanu and Stephenson (2022).
[2] Gunatilleke (2021).

framework to understand and evaluate these responses through the lens of freedom of expression.[3]

Discovering the roots of destructive propaganda is important because it provides insights into the motives and strategies, allows the development of countermeasures, safeguards democratic values, promotes dialogue and reconciliation, and strengthens media literacy. By understanding and addressing the roots of propaganda, we can mitigate its harmful effects and foster a more informed and resilient society. When the causes of the disease are known, it is easier to deal with the symptoms and take countermeasures. Next, the impact of the war on freedom of speech in Ukraine is presented.

Back in 1928, the British researcher A. Ponsonby, in his work "Falsehood in War Time", tried to inform society about the dangers of propaganda and the role of the mass media in controlling public opinion.[4] Wars resemble each other and propaganda during wars is similar. Ann Morelli, a professor of history from Brussels, analysed the mentioned work and concluded that the following "principles of military propaganda" are still relevant today:

(1) We do not want war;
(2) The enemy alone is to be blamed for the war;
(3) The enemy is inherently evil;
(4) We defend a noble cause, not our own interest;
(5) The enemy commits atrocities on purpose;
(6) The enemy uses illegal weapons;
(7) We suffer small losses, those of the enemy are enormous;
(8) Artists and intellectuals back our cause;
(9) Our cause is holy;
(10) Whoever doubts our propaganda is a traitor.[5]

Criminal liability is provided for in the Ukrainian criminal legislation for the spread of these types of propaganda.[6] The next section will look at the reaction of the Ukrainian legislator to such manifestations in more detail.

Social networks are full of posts about justifying war, glorifying the aggressor and inciting hatred on the basis of national, regional, racial or religious affiliations. Sociologists have long noticed that propaganda relies on already formed views. Each audience has its own preferences, unsatisfied interests and markers for identification. The echo chamber effect is particularly dangerous, and internet platforms contribute to the growth of the negative impact of this phenomenon. Propaganda is aimed at people who already sympathise with the ideas. The mass media controlled by the Russian government promote different narratives each aimed towards specific

---

[3] Bontcheva et al. (2020).

[4] Ponsonby (1971 [1928]).

[5] Anne Morelli: Die Prinzipien der Kriegspropaganda. https://www.deutschlandfunk.de/anne-morelli-die-prinzipien-der-kriegspropaganda-100.html. Accessed 26 May 2024.

[6] Mazepa (2023).

audiences.[7] It is well known that people prefer information that corresponds to their picture of the world. Those who find themselves in an information bubble[8] will be exposed to those aspects of events that are limited to that "bubble".[9]

Therefore, we can distinguish three directions of counteraction to destructive propaganda: (1) legislative; (2) technical and (3) cognitive. Of these, the legislative one is the formation of a clear legal framework with the help of civil and criminal law instruments regarding liability for the dissemination of illegal propaganda content and the creation and functioning of legal institutions to combat fakes, disinformation and propaganda. The technical direction consists in the use of information technologies and artificial intelligence. The cognitive direction of countering propaganda consists in the media literacy of the population and the development of critical thinking.

References

Anne Morelli: Die Prinzipien der Kriegspropaganda. https://www.deutschlandfunk.de/anne-morelli-die-prinzipien-der-kriegspropaganda-100.html. 26 May 2024

Bontcheva K et al (2020) Balancing act: countering digital disinformation while respecting freedom of expression. United Nations Educational, Scientific and Cultural Organization, Geneva, Switzerland

Gunatilleke G (2021) Justifying limitations on the freedom of expression. Human Rights Rev 22(1):91–108

Horun (2023) Zasady formuvannia vorozhoi propahandy ta zakhody protydii yii v umovakh voiennoho stanu v Ukraini (Principles of formation of hostile propaganda and measures to counteract it under the conditions of martial law in Ukraine). Informatsiia i pravo 2(45):163–171

Mazepa S (2023) Criminal law provisions countering propaganda on social media in connection with the Russo–Ukrainian war: OER Osteuropa Recht 68(4):443–456

Oates S (2016) Russian media in the digital age: propaganda rewired Russ Polit 1(4):398–417

Ponsonby A (1971 [1928]) Falsehood in wartime: containing an assortment of lies circulated throughout the nations during the great war. Garland Publishing, London

Rinceanu J, Stephenson R (2022) Eine diagnose digitaler Krankheiten. Max Planck Forschung 3:14–19

Seargeant P, Tagg C (2019) Social media and the future of open debate: a user-oriented approach to Facebook's filter bubble conundrum. Discour Context Media 27:41–48

---

[7] Oates (2016).
[8] Seargeant and Tagg (2019).
[9] Horun (2023).

Chapter 3
Ukraine's Reaction to Propaganda in Wartime Conditions

Propaganda has developed into an intricate web of hate speech, fakes and disinformation. In our previous study, we concluded that propaganda should be considered the dissemination of information and falsification for the purpose of manipulating the public consciousness and inciting others to perform illegal behaviour. In this study, we are talking only about destructive, illegal propaganda.[1]

The legislation of Ukraine contains a number of legal norms that limit the freedom of expression of views, due to the need to protect the national interests of Ukraine, its territorial integrity, ensuring law and order, etc.

Thus, hostile propaganda masquerades as "free speech" or "an alternative point of view." In Ukraine, the issue of combating propaganda seems to have always been relevant. However, special attention to counteracting this criminal phenomenon can be seen after the annexation of the Crimea and the Revolution of Dignity. In 2015, the "law on decommunisation" came into force which provided for distancing from the legacy of the USSR and the imposition of a Russian vision of Ukrainian history. This law also provided for criminal liability for the manufacture or distribution of communist or Nazi symbols and propaganda of communist and nationalist (Nazi) totalitarian regimes.[2] The next reaction was to ban the social networks Odnoklassniki and Vkontakte, with a number of sites with pro-Russian content also being blocked.[3]

Moreover, in the context of the full-scale invasion of the Russian Federation against Ukraine, a number of new types of propaganda have been criminalised, such as denying the ongoing war; justifying the invasion; glorifying the attackers; propaganda in educational institutions; hate speech based on regional affiliation (eastern and western parts of Ukraine). Public calls to oppose the lawful activities of the Armed Forces of Ukraine are also prohibited, as is calling on society to ignore mobilisation

---

[1] Mazepa (2024). Some research results were published in the mentioned article in Ukrainian.

[2] Mazepa (2022).

[3] Decision of the National Security and Defence Council of Ukraine of 28 April 2017 "On the Application of Personal Special Economic and Other Restrictive Measures (Sanctions)". https://zakon.rada.gov.ua/laws/show/n0004525-17#Text. Accessed 20 May 2024.

in wartime. Such statements are dangerous for the national security of the country and can strongly polarise society. The balance between free speech and the potential harm it can cause has long been critically debated in academia (Frederick 1982; Gey 2008; Weaver 2009; Oster 2021). In any case, denying or rewriting historical facts about genocide or wars is against the human rights convention and the ran counter to the fundamental values of the Convention, namely justice and peace (Garaudy 2003; Lehideux 1998).

Another step consisted of the adoption of a new Law "On the Media".[4] The old version of this law contained only a prohibition on calls in the media for violent regime change, the overthrow of constitutional order, the initiation or waging of an aggressive war or military conflict, the violation of the territorial integrity of Ukraine, or the end of the independence of Ukraine, along with a prohibition on spreading information that justifies or promotes such actions, spreading expressions that incite hatred, enmity or cruelty towards individuals or groups of persons on national, racial or religious grounds.

The new law adds to the above a prohibition on the media in Ukraine spreading information:

- that denies or justifies the criminal nature of the communist totalitarian regime of 1917–1991 in Ukraine, the criminal nature of the National Socialist (Nazi) totalitarian regime, or creates a positive image of anyone who held a leadership position in the Communist Party (the position of district committee secretary and above), the highest bodies of government and administration of the USSR, the Ukrainian SSR (USSR), other Union and autonomous Soviet republics (except for cases related to the development of Ukrainian science and culture), employees of Soviet state security bodies, justifies the activities of Soviet state security bodies, the establishment of Soviet power in Ukraine or in separate administrative-territorial units, the persecution of participants in the struggle for Ukraine's independence in the twentieth century. However, the distribution and showing of films containing the popularisation of Soviet state security bodies are regulated by the Law of Ukraine "On Cinematography"[5];
- containing the symbols of the communist or national socialist (Nazi) totalitarian regime, except for the cases stipulated by the Law of Ukraine "On the Condemnation of the Communist and National Socialist (Nazi) Totalitarian Regimes in Ukraine and Prohibition of Propaganda Using Their Symbols";
- containing the propaganda of the Russian totalitarian regime supporting the armed aggression of the Russian Federation as a terrorist state against Ukraine, as well as including the symbolism of the military invasion of the Russian totalitarian regime, except for the cases provided for by the Law of Ukraine "On the Prohibition of Propaganda of the Russian Nazi Totalitarian Regime, Armed Aggression of the Russian Federation as terrorist state against Ukraine, symbols of the military invasion of the Russian Nazi totalitarian regime in Ukraine";

---

[4] Law on the Media. https://zakon.rada.gov.ua/laws/show/2849-20#Text. Accessed 20 May 2024.

[5] Law on the cinematography (1998). https://zakon.rada.gov.ua/laws/show/9/98-%D0%B2%D1%80#Text. Accessed 25 May 2024.

- that humiliates or disparages the state language;
- that denies or calls into question the existence of the Ukrainian people (nation) and/or Ukrainian statehood and/or the Ukrainian language.

Further, using examples of specific cases, it will be considered how criminal law works to counter illegal propaganda in wartime conditions. The criminal provisions are of a blanket nature and refer to the legislation mentioned above.

References

Decision of the National Security and Defence Council of Ukraine of 28 April 2017 "On the Application of Personal Special Economic and Other Restrictive Measures (Sanctions)". https://zakon.rada.gov.ua/laws/show/n0004525-17#Text. Accessed 20 May 2024

Frederick S (1982) Free speech: a philosophical enquiry. Cambridge University Press, Cambridge, 81, 148, 162–163

Gey SG (2008) The first amendment and the dissemination of socially worthless untruths. Florida State Univ Law Rev 36

Garaudy v. France (2003) application No. 65831/01

Law on the cinematography (1998) https://zakon.rada.gov.ua/laws/show/9/98-%D0%B2%D1%80#Text Accessed 25 May 2024

Law on the Media (2023) https://zakon.rada.gov.ua/laws/show/2849-20#Text. Accessed 20 May 2024

Lehideux and Isorni v. France (1998) application No. 55/1997/839/1045, para. 47

Mazepa S (2022) Criminal law provisions countering propaganda on social media in connection with the Russo–Ukrainian war. German Legal J "Osteuropa Recht" 4

Mazepa S (2024) A dangerous combination of propaganda and the internet in the conditions of the Russian–Ukrainian war. Law of Ukraine. No. 1

Oster J (2021) 7 On "balancing" and "social watchdogs": the European court of human rights as a norm entrepreneur for freedom of expression. In: Callamard A, Bollinger L (eds) Regardless of frontiers: global freedom of expression in a troubled world. Columbia University Press, New York Chichester, West Sussex, 165–184 https://doi.org/10.7312/boll19698-010. Accessed 20 May 2024

Weaver RL, Delpierre N, Boissier L (2009) Holocaust Denial and governmentally declared 'truth': French and American perspectives. Texas Tech Univ Law Rev 41:495

Chapter 4
Ukrainian Cases on the Propaganda of Changing the Constitutional Order or State Borders

The Criminal Code of Ukraine establishes liability for criminal offences against the dissemination of propaganda that infringes on the foundations of national and public security, peace, the security of mankind and international law and order. In particular, it covers activities involving the production and (or) distribution of items considered as forms of propaganda. For this purpose, propaganda is considered to cover the distribution of materials: concerning forceful change or overthrow of the constitutional order or the seizure of state power (Article 109 Clause 2 of the Criminal Code of Ukraine); calling for change to the territorial boundaries or national borders of Ukraine (Article 110 Clause 1 of the Criminal Code of Ukraine); concerning encroachment on the territorial integrity and inviolability of Ukraine; concerning the distribution of materials calling for such actions (Article 110 Clause 1 of the Criminal Code of Ukraine); propaganda of terrorism (Article 258-2 of the Criminal Code of Ukraine); calling for actions that threaten public order—the production or distribution of materials with public calls for pogroms, arson, the destruction of property, seizure of buildings or structures, the forced eviction of citizens threatening public order (Article 295 of the Criminal Code of Ukraine); calling for a violation of citizens' equal rights based on their racial, ethnic or religious differences, disability for other characteristics (Article 161 of the Criminal Code); concerning genocide—the production and/or distribution of materials calling for genocide (Article 442 Clause 2 of the Criminal Code of Ukraine). In addition, there is Article 436-1 of the Criminal Code of Ukraine which makes the production, distribution and public use of communist, Nazi symbols and propaganda of communist and national socialist (Nazi) totalitarian regimes a criminal offence, along with calls justifying, recognising as legitimate or denying the armed aggression of the Russian Federation against Ukraine, or the glorification of its participants (Article 436-2 of the Criminal Code of Ukraine).

Mazepa (2024).

Article 10 of the European Convention for the Protection of Human Rights and Fundamental Freedoms guarantees the right to freedom of expression, which extends to anyone who wants to inform or to receive information, whether it is a scientist or a journalist, or the mass media in general. This freedom also applies to the dissemination of information on the internet and the expression of one's beliefs and opinions, as well as receiving and transmitting information without the intervention of state authorities and regardless of borders.

With this in mind, it is useful to analyse selected examples of propaganda aimed at changing the constitutional order or the national borders, how these offences are detected in social networks, how Ukrainian courts consider "likes" posted on social media and the spread of destructive propaganda on social network platforms like Facebook, Odnoklassniki, and Vkontakte.

Our research analysed judicial practice for the period from 1 January 2014 to 1 February 2023—during the war period—and involved a detailed analysis of criminal cases of certain categories from 2019, since access to full court decisions online using the Unified State Register of Court Decisions has only been possible since January 2019. One of the most widespread crimes that encroaches on the information security of Ukrainian society in the conditions of war is the distribution of illegal content aimed at violently changing or overthrowing the constitutional order or seizing state power. There were 100 verdicts made public (54 verdicts in the period 1 January 2014 to 31 December 2018 and 46 verdicts from 1 January 2019 to 23 February 2023)[1] concerning people charged with the distribution of illegal content, calls for action aimed at violent change or overthrowing of the constitutional order or for the seizure of state power—criminal offences under Article 109 of the Criminal Code of Ukraine. Several of these criminal cases are discussed in more detail below.

4.1 Court Judgments Declaring Propaganda Content as Criminal[2]

On the social networks Facebook, Odnoklassniki and Vkontakte, offenders posted the following messages:

> SANE PEOPLE, COME FORWARD! Great changes are in store for us this summer! It's time for us to start acting! Our Russian brothers are on our doorstep and will help us demolish the filth that is trying poorly to rule the GREAT Dnipropetrovsk Republic! The non-governor has already packed his bags and is preparing to go to his western LGBT brothers, so let's help him to do it faster! The people are tired of the fascist orders of the Kiev junta! With us, there are already more than a thousand military men who have refused to carry out the criminal orders of the fascists and kill our Russian brothers! THE DNIPROPETROVSK PEOPLE'S REPUBLIC TO BE! NOW THE QUESTION OF SUPPLYING US WITH WEAPONS FROM RUSSIAN BROTHERS IS ALREADY BEING RESOLVED, IF THERE IS ANY RESISTANCE FROM THE AUTHORITIES, WE WILL

---

[1] See the unified state register of court decisions: https://reyestr.court.gov.ua/.
[2] Mazepa (2024).

4.1 Court Judgments Declaring Propaganda Content as Criminal

GIVE A FULL-FLEDGED FIGHT BACK. My private box is open for anyone who wants to help liberate the great Dnipropetrovsk People's Republic! TOGETHER WE WILL NOT BE DEFEATED![3]

A user shared the following post on the social media network "Odnoklassniki":

Ukrainians! dear compatriots, brothers and sisters! Liberation is coming to us from the traitorous occupying Jews who have seized power in Ukraine. Brother Ukrainians, keep calm. record the crimes of the last days of Nazi power. Sisters, call your husbands, children and fathers. let them lay down their arms and return home, taking the occupying idiots in the person of the Zelensky government prisoner. everything will be fine, don't panic. the Russian world will win!

This same user also posted a video message from an unidentified person in military uniform with weapons and other military equipment, making the following speech:

I appeal to Ukrainian servicemen - We are not Americans and we are not bringing you democracy. If you have it, we will not touch it. Ukraine remains Ukrainian. In the near future, we will remove from power the regime that is selling you to foreigners. Don't waste your lives for this scum! Save them for your country and your loved ones! Don't touch us! And we won't touch you. You can't have a worse government than the current one. By calling Russia an enemy and getting cosy with NATO, they left us no choice. We are not the enemy. A little more, and you will be convinced of this.[4]

Another post on Odnoklassniki stated:

Dear compatriots, stop suffering the dominance of the bloodthirsty authorities of Kyiv! The oppression of Russian speakers in Ukraine must stop!!! Residents of Novorossiya RISE UP!!!! You have endured enough, we need to burn out the Ukro-fascists from our land! These Ukro-pedos are well organised with Western money, so you can't take them with your bare hands! We need Molotov cocktails and weapons! We will fight them with their own methods! We really are stronger!

Above the text of this post, the territory of Ukraine is depicted with the south-eastern regions depicted in the colours of the flag of the Russian Federation (white, blue and red), the northern regions in the colours of the flag of the Republic of Belarus (red and green) and the western regions in the colours of the flag of the Republic of Poland (red and white).[5]

For posting and spreading such messages, the accused received, in most cases, a year of conditional imprisonment. In one case, the offender received four years

---

[3] The unified state register of court decisions of Ukraine: The verdict of the Babushkinsyi district court of Dnipro of 8 February 2023. Case No. 932/7074/22. https://reyestr.court.gov.ua/Review/108890713. Accessed 1 May 2024.

[4] The unified state register of court decisions of Ukraine: The verdict of the Shostkinskyi city district court of the Sumy region of 24 January 2023. Case No. 589/2159/22. https://reyestr.court.gov.ua/Review/108731984. Accessed 1 May 2024.

[5] The unified state register of court decisions of Ukraine: The verdict of the Kyiv district court of Odessa of 13 September 2022. Case No. 947/20001/22. https://reyestr.court.gov.ua/Review/106194043. Accessed 1 May 2024.

imprisonment and the confiscation[6] of property for spreading misinformation among classmates, because he did not admit his guilt and behaved aggressively in the courtroom, shouting separatist calls. For the offence of hate speech involving calls for the overthrow of the constitutional order, the person was charged under Article 109 Clause 2—actions aimed at a violent change or overthrow of the constitutional order[7] or at the seizure of state power—of the Criminal Code of Ukraine and Article 161 Clause 2—a violation of the equality of citizens depending on their racial, national, regional affiliation, religious beliefs, disability and on other grounds—of the Criminal Code of Ukraine.

On the one hand, freedom of speech allows individuals to say offensive things and humiliate others, but on the other hand, criticism of the Maidan (Revolution of Dignity) and Ukrainians is criminally punishable hate speech. A journalist or blogger with thousands of followers can publicly incite others to ignore mobilisation and they can be punished for this.

4.2 Court Verdicts Where the Dissemination of Propaganda Content Was Justified[8]

Special attention should be paid to the verdict of the Illichiv city court in cases concerning criminal offences provided for in Article 109 Clause 2 and Article 436-1 Clause 1 of the Criminal Code of Ukraine—public calls for violent change or the overthrow of the constitutional order or for the seizure of state power, as well as the dissemination of materials with calls to commit such actions and the production, distribution and public use of symbols of communist or national socialist (Nazi) totalitarian regimes, including in the form of souvenir products, the public performance of anthems of the USSR, Ukrainian SSR (USSR), other allied and autonomous Soviet republics or their fragments on the entire territory of Ukraine, except for the cases provided for by Article 4, Clauses 2 and 3 of the Law of Ukraine "On Condemnation of Communist and National Socialist (Nazi) Totalitarian Regimes in Ukraine and Prohibition of Propaganda of Their Symbols".

One of the posts that the court looked at was the following:

> I don't know who this man is, but he said it well: – If Kyiv, the mother of Russian cities, prohibits the Russian language, then the mother has been occupied! It's time to liberate the mother of RUSSIAN cities from filthy sharovarniks,[9]

---

[6] The unified State Register of Court Decisions of Ukraine (2022) The verdict of the Khmelnytskyi city district court of 1 March 2022. Case No. 686/5200/22. https://reyestr.court.gov.ua/Review/103628707. Accessed 9 May 2024.

[7] The unified state register of court decisions of Ukraine: The verdict of the Kovel city district court of the Volyn region of 20 September 2020. Case No. 1-кп/159/360/20. https://reyestr.court.gov.ua/Review/91751963. Accessed 1 May 2024.

[8] Mazepa (2024).

[9] This term is used in Russia to insult the Ukrainian people. *Sharovarniki* comes from the word *sharovary*, the wide trousers of Ukrainian folk costume.

which contain public calls for the seizure of state power, namely calls for the violent removal of powers and liberation from the state power of Ukraine was in effect at the time the text was created.

The accused person had been registered as a user on the social network "Odnoklassniki" for a long time and used the social network to communicate with her friends, who were mostly the same age as her, connected by a common past, having been born and raised during the USSR. She found the above post, which had been written by an unknown author, and reshared it on the network to her friends.

She claims not to have understood what the author of the post meant by the phrase "It's time to liberate the Mother of Russian cities from sharovaniks," and she did not think about it herself. She claims to have merely liked the imagery of the statement, but had no intention of spreading any calls for the violent seizure of state power.

In this regard, the main evidence of the prosecution is the conclusion of the forensic linguistic examination, according to which the illocutionary form of the appeal, achieved through the participle "It's time" in combination with the infinitive "to liberate". Taking into account the meaning of the lexeme "liberate" and the microcontext of this post, the text contains a call for the violent removal of powers and the liberation of the state from the state power of Ukraine in force at the time the text was created (due to the use of the lexeme "Kyiv" and the use of metonymy and mentions of the whole of Ukraine). It also calls to liberate the state from nationalist-minded individuals ("filthy sharovarniks") who, according to the author of the text, have taken over Ukraine (through using the lexeme "Kyiv", the author, again, uses metonymy and mentions all of Ukraine), have banned the Russian language and are destroying their own people, i.e. taking into account the context of the state authorities of Ukraine acting at the time when the post was written.

At the same time, the expert's conclusion is based on the choice of meaning of the lexeme "liberates" precisely in this content of violence. In fact, the expert did not state in her conclusion that the specified text contains calls for the seizure of state power. When the witness was being heard by the court, the expert also did not make such unconditional statements.

The court drew attention to the fact that the specified text is built on metaphors: "mother has been occupied", "mother of Russian cities", "liberate the Mother of Russian cities." All this creates polysemy (ambiguity) in the perception of the content of the text under investigation. In addition, the phrase "sharovarniks," which the expert defines as an allusion to nationalist-minded individuals who allegedly seized power, is an allegory for an offensive definition of an abstract concept—Ukrainian nationalism.

At the same time, the real circumstances of political life that developed during 2014–2019 do not indicate that the power in Ukraine at that time belonged to nationalist-minded individuals, and the statement that it was forbidden to speak Russian in Kyiv is also untrue. Liberation of the state from "sharovarniks," which can be understood as the current government (according to the expert), does not rule out the possibility of implementing this in a non-violent way: through elections, the struggle of political parties and public activity to implement the conditions for a voluntary relinquishment of power, changes to the Constitution of Ukraine, etc.

As an example, in Ukraine in 2014, the public created conditions under which the president of Ukraine was removed from the post of head of the executive branch of government, but while preserving all the branches of government through subsequent democratic elections; in 2019, the president of Ukraine, by his Decree No. 303/2019 of 21 May 2019, prematurely terminated the powers of the Verkhovna Rada of Ukraine and called for extraordinary elections. All of these were actions that can be defined as the release of a certain branch of government from the individuals who headed it or were a part of it. Therefore, in general, the lexeme "liberates" is not the same as the lexeme "seizes".

The court considered that this analysis is based on obviously known and understandable circumstances, as well as on general linguistic concepts that do not require additional expert research. The presented text in metaphorical and allegorical forms actually has the appearance of expressing the author's own opinion regarding the characteristics of the current government in Ukraine, and is their subjective judgment regarding the need to change it.

In this regard, when evaluating the prosecution's evidence, the court applied the practice of the European Court of Human Rights regarding compliance with the requirements of the Convention on the Protection of Human Rights and Fundamental Freedoms. The fact that the conducted pre-trial investigation resulted in "state interference" in the exercise of freedom of expression does not contradict the Convention, as long as it meets the requirements of Article 10 § 2 of the Convention. It is, therefore, necessary to determine whether the interference was "prescribed by law" or whether it had aims or objectives that were legitimate within the meaning of Article 10 § 2 of the Convention and was "necessary in a democratic society" to achieve those aims or objectives.

Regarding the first two aspects, the court agreed with the prosecution that the investigation conducted is undeniably based on Article 109 of the Criminal Code of Ukraine; moreover, its purpose is to protect "national security interests" and there is no reason to assume that the investigation has any other purpose. Accordingly, the pre-trial investigation was "established by law" and had a legitimate purpose, in accordance with Article 10 § 2 of the Convention.

The question remains whether the intervention was "necessary in a democratic society" to achieve the above objective. The ECtHR, in the case "*Handyside v. the United Kingdom*" (*Handyside v. the United Kingdom*, complaint No. 5493/72, decision of 7 December 1976, paragraph 49[10]) indicated that freedom of expression is one of the fundamental foundations of a democratic society and one of the basic conditions for its development and the self-improvement of each individual. Article 10 § 2 refers not only to that "information" or those "ideas" that are obtained legally or are considered offensive or insignificant, but also those that cause offence or cause outrage. Such are the requirements of tolerance, pluralism and breadth of views, without which a "democratic society" is impossible (see also the decision in

---

[10] *Handyside v United Kingdom*, Merits, App No. 5493/72, A/24, [1976] ECHR 5, (1976) 1 EHRR 737, (1979) 1 EHRR 737, IHRL 14 (ECHR 1976), 7 December 1976, European Court of Human Rights [ECHR].

4.2 Court Verdicts Where the Dissemination of Propaganda Content Was ...

the case of *Castells v. Spain* of 23 April 1992, paragraph 42[11] and the decision in the case of *"The Observer and Guardian" v. the United Kingdom* of 26 November 1991, paragraph 59 a[12]). This means that every 'formality', 'condition', 'restriction' or 'sanction' applied to this area must be proportionate to the legitimate aim they pursue. From another point of view, any person, when exercising their right to freedom of expression, bears "duties and responsibilities", the degree of which depends on the situation and the technical means used.

In this regard, the court must find out whether these "restrictions" contributed to the "protection of national security interests," which would make them "necessary in a democratic society."

The above analysis by the court of the text of the unknown author testifies to the factual inconsistency of the characteristics of the power in force at the time, but at the same time to the subjectivity of the author's position, in view of the need to liberate the state from the power in force.

According to paragraph 46 of the decision of the ECtHR in the case of *Lingens v. Austria* (No. 12/1984/84/131, dated 8 July 1986[13]), facts and evaluative judgments should be carefully distinguished (author's italics). The existence of facts can be proven, but the truth of evaluative judgments cannot. As far as evaluative judgments are concerned, this requirement cannot be met and is a violation of the very freedom of opinion that is a fundamental component of the right guaranteed by Article 10 of the Convention.

Thus, the court reached the conclusion that defining the specified text of an unknown author as a call to seize state power, and accusing a person of taking actions to spread it, is an intervention that does not meet the set legitimate goal, and is therefore unnecessary.

The court takes into account the fact that the specified text was further distributed by the accused person on the Odnoklassniki social network by being reposted without any comment on her part. At the same time, the act of reposting cannot be taken as an unambiguous sign of support for its content. The function "repost" in the internet community of social networks can be understood as supporting the topic, or inviting discussion, or has the purpose of trolling, etc.

The prosecution did not prove to the court's satisfaction that the text is a call to seize state power, or that the distribution of this text is the distribution of materials with calls for the seizure of state power.

The ECtHR has repeatedly emphasised that the evaluation of evidence is guided by the criterion of proof "beyond a reasonable doubt." According to its well-established practice, proof can result from a set of signs or irrefutable presumptions regarding facts that are sufficiently weighty, clear and consistent with each other (see case

---

[11] *Castells v Spain*, Merits and just satisfaction, App No. 11798/85, A/236, (1992) 14 EHRR 445, IHRL 2936 (ECHR 1992), 23 April 1992, European Court of Human rights.

[12] *"Observer and Guardian v United Kingdom*, The Observer Ltd and others and 'Article ... IHRL 2952 (ECHR 1991), 26 November 1991, European Court of Human Rights.

[13] *Lingens v. Austria*, App No. 9815/82, Case No. 12/1984/84/131, A/103, [1986] ECHR 7, (1986) 8 EHRR 103, (1986) 8 EHRR 407, IHRL 58, 8 July 1986, European Court of Human Rights.

"*Ushakov and Ushakova v. Ukraine*", application No. 10705/12, dated 09/18/2015, para. 78[14]).

If a user clicks the button to share information on social networks, does that really mean that they support the information shared? The obvious answer is no, as it may be done with the intention of attracting public attention or inviting discussion.

According to the position of the Supreme Court of Justice of the Supreme Court, set out in the resolution dated 4 July 2018 (case No. 688/788/15-k, paragraphs 25 and 26), the obligation on the court to carry out a comprehensive and impartial investigation of all the circumstances of the case in this context means that in order to recognise guilt as proven beyond a reasonable doubt, the prosecution's version must explain all the circumstances established by the court that are relevant to the event that is the subject of the trial. The court cannot disregard that part of the evidence and the circumstances established on its basis only for the reason that they contradict the version of the prosecution. The presence of such circumstances for which the version of the prosecution cannot provide a reasonable explanation, or which indicate the possibility of another version of the incriminated event, is grounds for reasonable doubt in proving a person's guilt. To meet the standard of proof beyond a reasonable doubt, it is not enough that the prosecution's version is merely more likely than the defence's version. The legislature requires that any reasonable doubt in the version of events presented by the prosecution be rebutted by the facts established on the basis of admissible evidence, and the only version with which a reasonable and impartial person can explain all of the facts established in court is that a version of events that provides grounds for finding a person guilty of the charge.

In the case of "*Barberà, Messegué and Jabardo v. Spain,*" the European Court of Human Rights established that, "the principle of presumption of innocence requires, among other things, that, in the performance of their duties, judges should not start the trial with the preconceived notion that the defendant committed a crime, which he is accused of, the burden of proof lies with the prosecution, and any doubt must be interpreted in favour of the accused (the defendant)."[15]

According to Article 62 of the Constitution of Ukraine and Article 17 Clause 4 of the Criminal Procedure Code of Ukraine, any doubts regarding the proven guilt of a person are interpreted in favour of that person. In accordance with Article 373 Clause 3 of the Criminal Procedure Code of Ukraine, a guilty verdict cannot be based on assumptions and is adopted only on the condition that a person's guilt in committing a criminal offence is proven during the trial.

Taking into account the established circumstances, the court's decision was to acquit on the basis of the lack of evidence that the person's actions comprised the criminal offence provided for in Article 109 Clause 2 of the Criminal Code of Ukraine.

---

[14] *Ushakov and Ushakova v. Ukraine*, European Court of Human Rights.

[15] *Barberà, Messegué and Jabardo v. Spain*, the decision of 6 December 1988: 33, § 77.

4.3 Court Verdicts Against People Who Spread Communist Symbols

Many of the analysed offences are carried out with the "Touch VPN" extension activated and installed, which allows a person to log in and view information contained on blocked internet sites. Thus, a user on the internet social network "Odnoklassniki" used Strichka (in Engl. "line")—a public bulletin board—to repost publications (records and topics) with images in which the coat of arms of the USSR was reproduced: a combination of hammer and sickle; a five-pointed star; the USSR flag; a combination of a sickle, a hammer and a five-pointed star; as well as an image that commemorates the anniversaries of the October Revolution, Komsomol Day and the abbreviation of the All-Soviet Leninist Communist Youth Union (VLKSM).

According to Article 34 of the Constitution of Ukraine, everyone is guaranteed the right to freedom of thought and speech, and to the free expression of their views and beliefs. Everyone has the right to freely collect, store, use and disseminate information orally, in writing or in any other way, at their discretion.[16] The exercise of these rights may be limited by law in the interests of national security, territorial integrity or public order in order to prevent riots or crimes, protect public health, to protect the reputation or rights of other people, to prevent the disclosure of information obtained in confidence, or to maintain the authority and impartiality of justice.

Article 1, Clause 1, point 2 of the Law of Ukraine "On the Condemnation of Communist and National Socialist (Nazi) Totalitarian Regimes in Ukraine and Prohibition of Propaganda of Their Symbols"[17] (hereinafter the "Act") uses the term propaganda of Communist and National Socialist (Nazi) totalitarian regimes in the following sense: public denial, in particular through the mass media, of the criminal nature of the communist totalitarian regime of 1917–1991 in Ukraine or the national socialist (Nazi) totalitarian regime; the dissemination of information aimed at justifying the criminal nature of the communist and national socialist (Nazi) totalitarian regimes, the activities of Soviet state security bodies, the establishment of Soviet power in Ukraine or in separate administrative and territorial units; the persecution of participants in the struggle for the independence of Ukraine in the twentieth century; the production and/or distribution, as well as the public use of products containing symbols of the communist, national socialist (Nazi) totalitarian regimes.

According to of Article 1 Clause 4 (c) of the Act, images that include flags, symbols, icons or other paraphernalia, in which the combination of a sickle and a hammer, a sickle, a hammer and a five-pointed star, a plough is reproduced.

According to Article 4, Clause 1 of the Act, the production, distribution, as well as public use of symbols of the communist totalitarian regime, symbols of the National Socialist (Nazi) totalitarian regime, including in the form of souvenir products, the public performance of the anthems of the USSR, Ukrainian SSR (USSR), other Union

---

[16] Constitution of Ukraine (2016).
[17] The Law of Ukraine "On the Condemnation of Communist and National Socialist (Nazi) Totalitarian Regimes in Ukraine and Prohibition of Propaganda of Their Symbols" (2015). https://zakon.rada.gov.ua/laws/show/317-19#Text. Accessed 20 May 2024.

and Autonomous Soviet Republics or their fragments, are prohibited throughout Ukraine.

According to Clause 117 of the Joint Interim Conclusion of the European Commission "For Democracy through Law" (Venice Commission) No. 823/2015 and the Office of Democratic Institutions and Human Rights of the OSCE (OSCE/ODIHR) No. FOE-UKR/280/2015 (hereinafter the "Conclusion") dated 19 December 2015 regarding the Act, in cases where laws lead to restrictions on the freedom of expression or the freedom of association, such restrictions must meet the requirements of a three-pronged test, i.e. be established by law, pursue a legitimate goal and be necessary in a democratic society.

According to page 118 of the Conclusion, although the Act can be considered as pursuing legitimate goals, it is not precise and clear enough for a person to be able, with sufficient certainty, to predict in advance the legality or illegality of their actions and to prevent arbitrary interference from the state authorities.

At the same time, the decision of the Constitutional Court of Ukraine in the case based on the constitutional submission of 46 People's Deputies of Ukraine regarding the Act's compliance with the Constitution of Ukraine (constitutionality) dated 16 July 2019 No. 9-p/2019 [Case No. 1-24/2018(1919/17)] the Act was recognised as being constitutional.

According to Article 151-2 of the Constitution of Ukraine, decisions and conclusions adopted by the Constitutional Court of Ukraine are binding, final and cannot be appealed.

Thus, the court reached the conclusion that the person had committed the criminal offence provided for in Article 436-1 Clause 1 of the Criminal Code of Ukraine—the distribution or public use of symbols of the communist totalitarian regime.

References

Castells v Spain, Merits and just satisfaction, App No. 11798/85, A/236, (1992) 14 EHRR 445, IHRL 2936 (ECHR 1992), 23 April 1992, European Court of Human rights
Handyside v United Kingdom, Merits, App No. 5493/72, A/24, [1976] ECHR 5, (1976) 1 EHRR 737, (1979) 1 EHRR 737, IHRL 14 (ECHR 1976), 7 December 1976, European Court of Human Rights [ECHR]
Lingens v. Austria, App No. 9815/82, Case No. 12/1984/84/131, A/103, [1986] ECHR 7, (1986) 8 EHRR 103, (1986) 8 EHRR 407, IHRL 58
Mazepa S (2024) A dangerous combination of propaganda and the internet in the conditions of the Russian–Ukrainian war. Law of Ukraine. No. 1. Some research results were published in the mentioned article in Ukrainian
The Observer and Guardian v United Kingdom, The Observer Ltd. and others and Article ... IHRL 2952 (ECHR 1991), 26 Nov 1991, European Court of Human Rights
The unified state register of court decisions of Ukraine: the verdict of the Babushkinsyi district court of Dnipro of 8 February 2023. Case No. 932/7074/22. https://reyestr.court.gov.ua/Review/108890713. Accessed 1 May 2024
The unified state register of court decisions of Ukraine: the verdict of the Shostkinskyi city district court of the Sumy region of 24 January 2023. Case No. 589/2159/22. https://reyestr.court.gov.ua/Review/108731984. Accessed 1 May 2024

References

The unified state register of court decisions of Ukraine: the verdict of the Kyiv district court of Odessa of 13 September 2022. Case No. 947/20001/22. https://reyestr.court.gov.ua/Review/106 194043. Accessed 1 May 2024

The unified State Register of Court Decisions of Ukraine (2022). The verdict of the Khmelnytskyi city district court of 1 March 2022. Case No. 686/5200/22. https://reyestr.court.gov.ua/Review/103628707. Accessed 09 May 2024

The unified state register of court decisions of Ukraine: the verdict of the Kovel city district court of the Volyn region of 20 September 2020. Case No. 1-кп/159/360/20. https://reyestr.court.gov.ua/Review/91751963. Accessed 01 May 2024

Ushakov and Ushakova v. Ukraine, the European Court of Human Rights

Chapter 5
Hate Speech

Hate speech is an evaluative concept, since there is no universally recognised concept according to the principles of international law. The criteria for defining hate speech are also quite controversial, as international and regional documents provide for different standards. The European Commission has put forward a proposal that steps up efforts to tackle hatred in all its forms in the European Union. It is planning to do so by reinforcing action across a variety of policies, including security, digital, education, culture and sport. This includes:

- more money towards protecting people and the places in which they worship
- a new code of conduct on countering illegal hate speech online
- engaging society as a whole to ensure the various initiatives at EU level can reach their full potential.

Respect and tolerance are founding values of our societies. More than that, the unique diversity we have within the EU, is a core part of our European identity. It is only by working together that we will protect these values and preserve our identity. The Commission is therefore also calling on EU institutions, Member States, civil society organisations and other partners to join forces in this fight.[1]

"Hate speech" covers words and phrases that reveal social tension around sensitive topics in the media space. An analysis of example material revealed that the topics of the Russian-Ukrainian war, internally displaced persons, national groups, people with drug addiction and those without housing are the most acutely presented.[2] Today, Ukrainian law deals with hate speech in the Law "On Information" as a component of the "inadmissibility of abusing the right to information." It considers hate speech to include: calls for the overthrow of the constitutional system, calls for the territorial

---

[1] No place for hate: a Europe united against hatred. https://commission.europa.eu/news/no-place-hate-europe-united-against-hatred-2023-12-06_en. Accessed 10 May 2024.
[2] Leptuga (2019).

integrity of Ukraine to be violated; propaganda of war, violence and brutality; calls to incite ethnic, racial and religious enmity; and calls to carry out terrorist acts.[3]

The objects of hate speech in Ukraine during the war are immigrants from the east and believers. Many materials are about "separatists" who called for and promoted "Russian peace." The language of hostility is also aimed at the Crimean Tatar community, Roma and Jews. The local press often used the language of hostility towards residents of other regions. Law No. 2110-IX dated 3 March 2022 entered into force on 16 March 2022. The legislator included signs of regional affiliation in the context of hate speech. A draft law (No. 5102) was registered in the Verkhovna Rada of Ukraine on 18 February 2021, and was in the state of "provided for review" for more than a year. Over the course of two days[4] in March 2022, it was considered by the committees of the Verkhovna Rada and adopted in full without any amendments. There are many discussions in scientific circles regarding the concept of region and its ambiguity in legislation.

There is a lot of hate speech content on social networks. Indeed, expressions of hatred on the internet can be defined through the categories of cyberhate and cyberbullying, which essentially encompass the category of hate speech broken down into its spatial expression. It is worth considering the language of hostility through the prism of the recent global problem—the outbreak of COVID-19. In early February 2020, four racist incidents related to the coronavirus outbreak were recorded and investigated by North Yorkshire Police in Great Britain; China's ambassador to the UK condemned the "hate" towards the Chinese after the outbreak.[5,6,7] Despite only four confirmed cases of COVID-19 in the UK at that time, the Chinese community noted a markedly racist response to the global health crisis; Manchester's Chinese Centre received numerous complaints about racist incidents involving children in schools across the region.[8] Thus, cases of hate speech based on belonging to the nation in which the virus was first detected caused a wave of hatred for a specific social group caused by the fear of infection. This resulted in cases of aggression towards representatives of the specified group. The feeling of fear of infection with COVID-19 is reinforced by messages received from the media, which can provoke an extremely unpredictable reaction in consumers of such information. Ukrainians

---

[3] Law on Information. https://zakon.rada.gov.ua/laws/show/2657-12?find=1&text=%D0%BC%D0%BE%D0%B2%D0%B0+%D0%BE%D1%80%D0%BE%D0%B6%D0%BD%D0%B5%D1%87%D1%96#w2_1. Accessed 10 May 2024.

[4] Khavroniuk (2022).

[5] North Yorkshire Police probe racist coronavirus-related incidents. BBC: https://www.bbc.com/news/uk-england-york-north-yorkshire-51407641. Accessed 25 May 2024.

[6] Chinese in UK report 'shocking' levels of racism after coronavirus outbreak. The Guardian: https://www.theguardian.com/uk-news/2020/feb/09/chinese-in-uk-report-shocking-levels-of-racism-after-coronavirus-outbreak. Accessed 25 May 2024.

[7] Xu et al. (2021).

[8] Holovko (2021).

evacuated from China were taken to a sanatorium in Novy Sanzhary, amid shouts of protesters and stones thrown at the buses.[9]

Thus, the European practice of developing criteria for identifying and identifying hate speech as having caused or with a high probability of causing hate crimes comes to the rescue. The Rabat action plan,[10] regarding the prohibition on propaganda of national, racial or religious hatred, seems to be the most important. This document provides three approaches:

- hate speech as a criminal offence (criminal liability);
- hate speech that does not pose a criminal threat, but may cause a reaction in the form of a civil lawsuit or administrative sanction (civil, administrative, property liability);
- hate speech that does not give rise to legal liability, as it is not provided for by law, but which causes concern about the threat of tolerance, goodwill and respect for the rights of other people.

Expressions of hate on social media networks became more relevant with the war. The phenomenon of echo cameras on online platforms deserves special attention. It was already mentioned in previous chapters that propaganda during the war often contains the language of hostility.

It is clear that, suppressing hate speech with the help of the Criminal Code is the last measure in the state's arsenal. Therefore, it is important to highlight the positive experience of Germany (regarding Facebook, etc.).[11] However for lawyers, judicial practice will be important, namely how the courts define hate in Germany.

When balancing interests in multipolar private legal relations, it is necessary to take into account the interests of other users during the discussion. A democratic culture of opinion fades when only the loud and the rude can assert themselves. Criminal law is the ultimatum of the constitutional state, so it can only define the extreme limit of what may be said. Therefore, there is a justified need to be able to prohibit the expression of certain opinions on platforms in cases where human rights or criminal law norms have not been violated.[12]

The European Union has been actively fighting hate speech on social media networks for a long time.[13] Germany is at the forefront of anti-hate organisation on online platforms. It is also important to cite court decisions that contain the specific details considered in such cases.

---

[9] Buses with evacuated Ukrainians from China arrived in Novi Sanzhary and were stoned (video) (2020). https://www.unian.ua/society/10883918-evakuyovanih-z-kitayu-ukrajinciv-dopravili-v-novi-sanzhari-avtobusi-zakidali-kaminnyam-video.html. Accessed 10 May 2024.

[10] Human Rights Council. Twenty-second session Agenda. Annual report of the United Nations High Commissioner for Human Rights and reports of the Office of the High Commissioner and the Secretary-General from 11 January 2013. The Office of the High Commissioner for Human Rights (UN Human Rights). https://www.ohchr.org/Documents/Issues/Opinion/SeminarRabat/Rabat_draft_outcome.pdf. Accessed 13 May 2024.

[11] Guggenberger (2017a).

[12] Raue and Trier (2022).

[13] Alkiviadou (2019).

Hate speech covers a wide range of expressions in a number of diverse contexts: open calls for discrimination against a certain social group, unjustified mentions of this group in a negative context, accusations of a group having a negative impact on the state of society, etc. The use of these expressions can be intentional or careless. Accordingly, the social consequences of such statements are also different. Considering this, it is possible to single out hate, slander, insult, fakes and propaganda as degrees of hate speech. A characteristic of hate speech is that it is applied to a person or group based on who they are. For example, if one person responded rudely to another in public transport because he was pushed, this is an insult. But if, in the same situation, a person uses discriminatory expressions regarding the identity of this person or the group to which they belong, or incites others to discriminate against this person or their group, then this is already hate speech.

The "Bez kordoniv" project, run by the public organization "Sotsialna Dija,"[14] monitored instances of racial and ethnic hostility or intolerance in the Ukrainian segment of the internet. In doing so, it adopted the definition of hate speech from the "Sova" Centre and, with minor modifications, also utilized the hate speech classification scale and monitoring methodology developed by the Centre's researchers. This scale of types of hate speech starts from the harshest forms, such as calls to enmity, violence and discrimination, ending with the denial of citizenship (referring to Ukrainian citizens as foreigners based on their ethnic identification) and references to ethnicity or citizenship in criminal records when this is not unavoidable, an integral part of the picture of a criminal incident.

In the conditions of Russian aggression, cases of inciting national and religious enmity and hatred, committed both by citizens of Ukraine, foreigners and representatives of the Russian Orthodox Church and its part of the Ukrainian Orthodox Church, became commonplace. Russia's special services also influence the destabilisation of Ukraine through the church. This has been confirmed by convictions against clergymen of the Russian Orthodox Church, in particular under Article 161 of the Criminal Code of Ukraine—"Violation of the equality of citizens depending on their racial, national, regional affiliation, religious beliefs, disability and other grounds."[15] In 2022, the Security Services of Ukraine began complex counter-intelligence and security measures (more than 40) in the environment of the Ukrainian Orthodox Church, which took place to stop the destructive activities of the pro-Russian clergy. As a result of measures taken by the Security Service of Ukraine, 61 criminal proceedings were initiated against 61 clergymen.[16] An unconditional guarantee for the successful process of bringing the perpetrators to criminal liability is the correct interpretation[17] and application of the provisions of Article 161 of the Criminal Code.

---

[14] Project "Without Borders" of the NGO "Social Action Center": Report on the results of monitoring of hate speech in the Ukrainian media (2014). K., 2015: 78.

[15] Criminal Code of Ukraine (2001). https://zakon.rada.gov.ua/laws/show/2341-14#Text. 25 May 2024.

[16] The Security Service of Ukraine served a notice of suspicion to Metropolitan Pavlo of the Ukrainian Orthodox Church (Moscow Patriarchate). https://ssu.gov.ua/novyny/sbu-povidomyla-pro-pidozru-mytropolytu-upts-mp-pavlu-video. Accessed 3 May 2024.

[17] Sharmar and Osoblyvosti (2023).

Any actions (public speeches, distribution of materials in mass communication media, etc.) that are carried out with the aim of spreading among certain groups of the population, feelings of hostility, enmity and disgust towards other ethnic or racial groups or denominations in order to cause others to have the same feelings and attitudes towards such groups, their way of life, culture, customs, religion, denigration of the positive qualities of that or another nation on an equal footing with others should be considered a violation of the equality of citizens. These can be: public incitement to expel representatives of relevant ethnic or racial groups or groups that live compactly in a separate region from the borders of Ukraine, or resettle them to other regions; the distribution of materials with known false information (fakes) about such groups; propaganda involving racial, regional, national, religious exclusivity or intolerance; violations of historical and cultural monuments or other values, or their destruction or damage, etc. Actions aimed at inciting national, regional, racial or religious enmity and hatred, at humiliating national honour and dignity combined with a justification or recognition as legitimate, the denial of armed aggression of the Russian Federation against Ukraine, the glorification of its participants, must also be qualified under Article 436-2 of the Criminal Code of Ukraine.

5.1 Some Ukrainian Cases Involving Hate Speech

This subsection looks at a number of verdicts of Ukrainian courts that were passed during the war. It is often observed that hate speech goes hand in hand with the justification of war, the glorification of the aggressor with calls to change the constitutional order. On the basis of a semantic analysis, it was established which statements are criminally punishable.[18] For example, many judgments were passed against clerics

---

[18] In "The Orthodox Church of Ukraine: Steps Towards Autocephaly" (2019) Victoria Mikhailovna Bokoch writes "One of the problems of religious and church life in Ukraine that has long remained relevant and needed to be addressed was the problem of the unity and independence of the Orthodox Church. After all, since the baptism of Rus, Ukrainian Orthodoxy was under the jurisdiction of either the Constantinople or Moscow Patriarchates and did not have its own independent existence. In addition, the political and religious vicissitudes of Ukraine's history have led to a church split, which has had a negative impact not only on the religious and church aspects, but also on the state of Ukrainian society. Repeated attempts by the Ukrainian political and church elite to overcome the division of Orthodoxy and achieve autocephaly have long been unsuccessful. However, on 5 January 2019, Ecumenical Patriarch Bartholomew signed the Tomos of Autocephaly of the Orthodox Church of Ukraine in Istanbul and handed it to Metropolitan Epifaniy the next day. Thus, the dramatic long-term confrontation between pro-Ukrainian and pro-Russian political and church forces in Ukraine and abroad, the struggle between supporters and opponents of church independence, ended with the unification of churches, the creation of the OCU and its autocephalous status. Autocephaly was not just "granted" by the Patriarchate of Constantinople to this church, but with the help of Ecumenical Patriarch Bartholomew, it was "won" in the difficult struggle of Ukrainian national-patriotic political and religious forces against Russian and pro-Russian ones. Since church independence is on a par with the independence of the Ukrainian state, not only Orthodox hierarchs but also representatives of the Ukrainian authorities contributed to its achievement, and their actions helped to resolve a problem

in churches. In church groups on social media, there were publications with negative information about the Orthodox Church of Ukraine.

These posts were deliberately offensive, questioning the authorities of the church and disparaging the church itself, in attempts to convince believers of their own inferiority in relation to what the poster apparently believed was the more ancient church. These posts used quotation marks freely: "Ukrainian autocephaly", "great" goal, "Pseudo-church organisation under the name "Orthodox Church of Ukraine" to show that these names are given with a hint of ironic attitude, which can cause offence to the church followers.[19]

A priest in the men's monastery, whose profile photo shows the words "Who rules in Ukraine?", commented "It's time to end the Chabadniks," in which there is a statement, expressed in the form of a direct appeal to an unspecified number of addressees, with a call to end the activities of the Chabadniks, the Jewish group that the posted claims usurped power in Ukraine.[20]

In the resulting court case, the verdict,[21] presented below, found that the post in question was a clear attempt to justify the armed aggression of the Russian Federation against Ukraine:

- the statement that the occupation of Crimea by the Russian Federation is a necessary step in order to prevent NATO forces from entering the peninsula. The legitimate informational impact of justifying the armed aggression of the Russian Federation against Ukraine by repeating the narrative of Russian propaganda that the occupation of Crimea is a forced action in response to the aggressive actions of NATO, and that, if the troops of the Russian Federation had not entered Crimea, then the peninsula would have been captured by NATO troops;
- the statement that Donbas has always been "Russian" and that Ukrainians ("*Khokhly*") have no claim to this region of Ukraine. The legitimate informational impact of justifying the armed aggression of the Russian Federation against Ukraine by repeating the typical narratives of Russian propaganda that all of Ukraine, or certain parts of it, are "originally Russian lands" forming the historical lands of the Russian Federation on which "Russians" supposedly live (while Ukrainians have no claim to these lands) and which the Russian Federation should return to its composition in order to restore "historical justice" and protect the "Russians" in these territories.

---

that had long troubled not only the religious and church environment but also the Ukrainian state and society. There are Ukrainian Orthodox Church and Orthodox Church of Ukraine in Ukraine.".

[19] The unified state register of court decisions of Ukraine: The verdict of the Amur-Nyzhniodniprovskyi district court of Dnipro 21 August 2023, case No. 199/6598/23. https://reyestr.court.gov.ua/Review/112928118. Accessed 10 May 2024.

[20] The unified state register of court decisions of Ukraine: The verdict of the Beregivskyi district court of the Zakarpatyya region 29 June 2023. Case No. 297/1824/23. https://reyestr.court.gov.ua/Review/111995302. Accessed 1 May 2024.

[21] The unified state register of court decisions of Ukraine: The verdict of the Lubomlskyi district court of the Volyn region 13 June 2023. Case No. 163/1079/23. https://reyestr.court.gov.ua/Review/111543461. Accessed 01 May 2024.

- the use of the ethnophilism "*Khokhol*" in relation to Ukrainians, which is evidence of a negative, hostile, contemptuous attitude towards the citizens of Ukraine and people of Ukrainian nationality. According to the dictionary interpretation, the word "*Khohol*" is a derogatory name for a Ukrainian, used to express contempt for citizens of Ukraine and people of Ukrainian nationality, to humiliate and insult them as representatives of a certain nation and state.

Another case concerns the church's distribution of hostile propaganda literature. Photos of a gathering of clergy, led by the head of the Kirovohrad Diocese of the Ukrainian Orthodox Church, downloading and printing the following books of the Russian publishing house were posted on Facebook:

1. "Russian Church on the Guard of Orthodoxy in the 21st Century" (Russian);
2. "Contribution to the Dialogue on Ukrainian Autocephaly" (Russian);
3. "Ukrainian church question" (Russian);
4. "Contemporary Ukrainian issues" (Russian);
5. "Church Rules and Church Unity" (Russian).

On the "Odnoklassniki" platform was a post saying:

UNLEASH DONBASS'S HANDS. LET THEM DEAL WITH KYIV. FOR THOSE WHO HAVE BEEN SHOT, FOR THOSE PRISONERS WHO HAVE BEEN TORTURED, FOR ALL THOSE WHO WILL NEVER RETURN.

In the circumstances of the Russian invasion of Ukraine, this public post on the internet was deemed to contain a public call for a violent change in the constitutional system and the seizure of state power in Ukraine. The call is achieved by writing the post in the "imperative form".

At the same time, the poster uses the words "*zapadensky*" and "*Khokhly*", which is characteristic of Russian propaganda narratives and has a negative expressive evaluation in combination with the abusive word "cattle". *Zapadenets* is an offensive name for Ukrainians, meaning belonging to the west of Ukraine. Posting a set of contemptuous, disparaging statements about Ukraine is a sign of purposeful incitement of enmity on national soil. The widely circulated guilty text document contains an insult to the national anthem of Ukraine by distorting its content.[22]

The following case was exposed in Kalush, on the Odnoklassniki platform:

ESPECIALLY FOR THOSE POT-HEADED UKRAINIANS AND KHOKHOLS WHO VISIT MY PAGE! WANT TO KNOW MY POSITION? I AM FOR THE MILITIA! FOR DONBASS! FOR LUHANSK AND DONETSK AND I ALSO BELIEVE THAT THE CRIMEA IS RUSSIA! I RESPECT VLADIMIR PUTIN! I AM AGAINST GENOCIDE AND MURDER!

The priest who posted this statement, positioning himself as a servant of God who must convey the truth to followers of the relevant religious community, publicly conveyed information using methods of deception and manipulation with the aim of

---

[22] The unified state register of court decisions of Ukraine: The verdict of the Kalush city district court of the Ivano-Frankivsk region. Case No. 345/1885/23. https://reyestr.court.gov.ua/Review/110558242. Accessed 1 May 2024.

strengthening the hostile attitude of church visitors to Jews. Among other things, he tried to demonstrate a contemptuous and humiliating attitude towards the Ukrainian people and glorified the Russian people, while also aggressively imposing of his own religious beliefs and worldview, thereby inciting national enmity and hatred, as well as degrading the national honour and dignity of Ukrainians and Jews.[23]

In another criminal case, next person posted the following text on the social media network Odnoklassniki:

> The authorities of the Zaporozhye region have announced their intention to join Russia!!! Zaporozhye region, after its complete liberation from Ukra inian nationalists, will take a course to join Russia as a full-fledged entity. Vladimir Rogov, a member of the main council of the military-civil administration of the region, told RIA Novosti. 'The future of the Zaporozhye region can only be one thing – we must be part of Russia, must become a full-fledged subject of the Russian Federation. We don't need grey areas, we don't need the Zaporozhian People's Republic. We want to be a part of Russia, as we always have been for hundreds of years,' Rogov said. And ends with the following: 'Ukrainian nationalists also understand that they will not hold Zaporozhye, so they are already withdrawing their assets from the city and evacuating their families. Everything leads to the fact that the city will be liberated.'
>
> And here is Ukraine? The first thing I discovered for myself is that I really don't know the history of the country in which I lived for 23 years. To my surprise, our flag turned out to be someone else's flag, and the anthem – stolen from the Poles 'Poland is not dead yet.' The history of 'ancient' Ukraine is a twisted, stolen, thousand-year history. After all, before the revolution of 1917, neither such a state nor such a nationality had ever existed for centuries. But only the border strip of territory between Russia and Poland was called the outskirts, and in Polish, Ukrainy. And since for some time the border ran along the Dnieper, the adjacent lands were called the right-bank and left-bank outskirts-Ukraine. The Little Russians themselves and their land were always called only Russian...
>
> DEAR RUSSIAN WARRIORS! ODESSA REJOICES AT EVERY EXPLOSION! WE ARE READY TO RECEIVE DEATH... JUST SO THAT FOOLS WITH TORCHES DO NOT MARCH THROUGH OUR RUSSIAN LAND, SO THAT OUR CHILDREN DO NOT BECOME SODOM! WE BOW LOW TO YOU FROM ORTHODOX ODESSA!

with a graphic image of the inscription on the wall "Odessa–Russian city", which is aimed glorifying the people who carried out the armed aggression of the Russian Federation against Ukraine, which began in 2014.

In all of the cases mentioned above, the posters were found guilty and received sentences involving conditional imprisonment.

---

[23] The unified state register of court decisions of Ukraine: The verdict of the Krasnogvardiyskyi district court of Dnipropetrovsk, July 2010. Case No. 204/3352/22. https://reyestr.court.gov.ua/Review/10506082. Accessed 1 May 2024.

5.2 Some German Cases About Hate Speech

For comparison, several German cases are presented, showing how German courts define content as illegal. Since the research was conducted at the German University of Osnabrück, the author had the opportunity to get acquainted with the judicial practice of Germany.

The first proceedings that will be looked at involved an NPD (Nationaldemokratische Partei Deutschlands—National Democratic party of Germany) election ad that the broadcaster ZDF[24] had refused to show. It depicts a black-grey background in front of which blood spatters run down the screen; there are the sounds of a gun being loaded and a shot. Crime scenes and the names of victims of homicides and other violent crimes are faded in faster and faster. This sequence is accompanied by the spoken text: "Since the arbitrary opening of the border in 2015 and the uncontrolled mass immigration Germans become victims of foreign knifemen almost every day. Migration kills!" It claims that many cities and districts have meanwhile become "no-go areas" for Germans.[25] Since the state looks the other way or is unable to act, the NPD itself took the initiative with a protection zone campaign. The core of the spot is the statement that foreigners—especially those who have entered the country since 2015—are all dangerous criminals who pose an acute threat to the life and limb of the German population. The term "knifemen" is not limited to the individual perpetrators associated with the displayed names of the victims and crime scenes. The combination with the phrase "Migration kills" results in the statement "Kill migrants." In this way, foreigners, i.e. part of the population, would be violated in their human dignity by being maliciously made contemptible. The election commercial could also be accused of disturbing public peace. By propagating what it terms protection zones, which would be secured by uniformed units, the state's monopoly on the use of force is called into question and arbitrary and violent action against parts of the population is suggested. The BVerfG (Bundesverfassungsgericht—Federal Constitutional Court of Germany) rejected an urgent application for compulsory broadcasting, as the OVG (Oberverwaltungsgericht—the Higher Administrative Court) did not misjudge the protective content of the freedom of expression under Article 5 para. 1 S. 1 GG (Grundgesetz für die Bundesrepublik Deutschland—Basic Law for the Federal Republic of Germany—the constitution).[26]

However, after revising the election advert, the Federal Constitutional Court issued interim order 19 obliging ZDF to broadcast it. Because the focus of the advert was amended to be now on the "victims," the only abstract threats mentioned are the "opening of borders" and "mass immigration. Therefore, no evident violation of criminal provisions was found.

---

[24] ZDF (Zweite Deutsche Fernsehen) is one of the largest public broadcasting organisations in Europe. It is based in Mainz. https://www.zdf.de/.

[25] Germans fear the rise of 'lawless' neighbourhoods, poll shows (2018). https://www.dw.com/en/germans-fear-the-rise-of-lawless-neighborhoods-poll-shows/a-43395944. Accessed 1 May 2024.

[26] Basic Law for the Federal Republic of Germany (the constitution). https://www.gesetze-im-internet.de/gg/BJNR000010949.html. Accessed 1 May 2024.

On the one hand, KG20 (Supreme court decision), in civil proceedings regarding the deletion of a video posted on YouTube—"Flensburg perpetrator 'refugee' from Eritrea, by the AfD (Alternative für Deutschland) parliamentary group in the Bundestag" decided that the video did not use the relevant term "knife immigration" as hate speech according to §130 para. 1 No. 2 StGB, and therefore was not considered illegal content according to §1 para. 3 NetzDG (the Network Enforcement Act).[27] An attack on human dignity (iSv §130 para. 1 No. 2 StGB) requires an attack against the victim's personality, against their humanity as such. The decision was that this cannot be determined in this case.

The Munich Higher Regional Court, on the other hand, confirmed the rejection of an application for an injunction against the blocking of a social media account. The website in question suggests to readers that government policy means German citizens are being deprived of their homes and properties, in order to make them available to migrants, on whom large amounts of tax proceeds are also being spent. The repeated designation as "illegal", along with other, more drastic formulations, give the impression that the refugees and asylum seekers are all staying in Germany illegally and are committing drug, sexual or violent offences here. The claim is that this would lead to "genocide" or the "abolition of one's own people According to the court, under Article 5 para. 1 S, 1 GG, is possible to make a post criticising a specific, actual or alleged practice of municipal and immigration policy, but not to post an incitement to hatred, according to §130 para. 2 No. 1 letter a StGB, which the accused made publicly available by reposting the offending post. This means that there is also illegal content in the sense of §1 para. 3 NetzDG.[28]

5.3 NetzDG

Germany is one of the Member States of the European Union that is successfully combatting online hate speech. A real breakthrough came with the adoption of the Law on Network Enforcement (NetzDG) in 2017.[29] Scientists have explored problematic issues connected with the operation of this law.[30] The essence of the legislative proposal is the obligation to create a procedure ensuring that—in response to a complaint—clearly illegal content is blocked or removed within 24 h and all illegal content is blocked or removed within seven days. NetzDG's work is essentially based on collaboration between the government, platforms and users. Social networks such as Facebook, Twitter and YouTube must create mechanisms whereby they can accept reports from users about illegal content. Next, the platforms must review

---

[27] Social Media Enforcement Improvement Act (the Network Enforcement Act—NetzDG). https://www.gesetze-im-internet.de/netzdg/BJNR335210017.html. Accessed 1 May 2024.

[28] https://www.gesetze-im-internet.de/netzdg/BJNR335210017.html. Accessed 1 May 2024.

[29] BMJ, Pressemitteilung v. 5.4.2017, https://www.bmjv.de/SharedDocs/Artikel/DE/2017/040 52017_NetzDG.html. Accessed 1 May 2024.

[30] Guggenberger (2017b).

each message and decide whether to remove it. If the platform does not remove the content within 24 h, it could be subject to a fine of up to 50 million euros. Contrary to the explanatory note to the law, setting a time limit for removal, which is already contrary to European law, does not prevent the "cooling effect."[31] Transparency reports published to date show that most content removal decisions are made within 24 h.[32]

For content to be removed, it must be deemed illegal under criminal law. There is a good deal of discussion in academic circles about how social media providers should properly evaluate the subjective facts of these criminal offences and offer possible justifications.[33] There is also the question of whether this will lead to internet platform providers being excessive about blocking content in order to avoid possible fines. In addition, the decision is not made against the user, but only against the network operator. The user is not necessarily connected to the content itself.

It is very important to strike a balance between protecting the fundamental right to freedom of speech and preventing hate on social media.[34]

If there are any doubts, the decision must be made in favour of freedom of expression. German judicial practice shows clearly how attacks on freedom of speech are punished. In a decision dated 10 September 2018,[35] the Frankfurt Regional Court ruled that weighing mutual interests in individual cases means that speech generally covered by freedom of expression can also be deleted. This occurs when a social media platform removes (still acceptable) hate speech "because such speech may significantly harm the interests of the platform provider, which is also focused on fact-based debate and promoting free speech for all users."[36]

Studying the German approach and the German experience will be useful when looking at the situation in Ukraine, since there are agreements between law enforcement agencies and social networks that have already resulted in fruitful cooperation. A Europe-wide unified law is needed to combat hate speech, fakes and propaganda.

References

Alkiviadou N (2019) Hate speech on social media networks: towards a regulatory framework? Inf Commun Technol Law 28(1):19–35

Basic Law for the Federal Republic of Germany. https://www.gesetze-im-internet.de/gg/BJNR000010949.html. Accessed 1 May 2024

BMJ, Pressemitteilung v. 5.4.2017. https://www.bmjv.de/SharedDocs/Artikel/DE/2017/04052017_NetzDG.html

---

[31] NetzDG RegE: 24.

[32] BMJ, Pressemitteilung v. 5.4.2017. Abrufbar unter: https://bmjv.de/SharedDocs/Artikel/DE/2017/04052017_NetzDG.html.

[33] Wimmers/Heymann, AfP 2017: 93 (94 f.).

[34] Heereman and Selzer (2019).

[35] LG Frankfurt/M. v. 10.9.2018—2-03 O 310/18, MMR 2018: 770.

[36] Keller (2018).

Buses with evacuated Ukrainians from China arrived in Novi Sanzhary and were stoned (video) (2020). https://www.unian.ua/society/10883918-evakuyovanih-z-kitayu-ukrajinciv-dopravili-v-novi-sanzhari-avtobusi-zakidali-kaminnyam-video.html. Accessed 10 May 2024

Chinese in UK report 'shocking' levels of racism after coronavirus outbreak. The Guardian. https://www.theguardian.com/uk-news/2020/feb/09/chinese-in-uk-report-shocking-levels-of-racism-after-coronavirus-outbreak. Accessed 24 May 2024

Criminal Code of Ukraine (2001). https://zakon.rada.gov.ua/laws/show/2341-14#Text

LG Frankfurt/M. v. 10.9.2018—2-03 O 310/18, MMR 2018, 770

Germans fear the rise of 'lawless' neighbourhoods, poll shows (2018). https://www.dw.com/en/germans-fear-the-rise-of-lawless-neighborhoods-poll-shows/a-43395944. Accessed 24 May 2024

Guggenberger N (2017a) Das Netzwerkdurchsetzungsgesetz in der Anwendung. Neue Juristische Wochenschrift: NJW 70(36):2577–2581

Guggenberger N (2017b) Das Netzwerkdurchsetzungsgesetz–schön gedacht, schlecht gemacht. Zeitschrift für Rechtspolitik 50(H.4):98–101

Heereman W, Selzer A (2019) Löschung rechtskonformer Nutzerinhalte durch Soziale Netzwerkplattformen—Ein Überblick am Beispiel von Facebook. Computer und Recht 35(4):271–276

Holovko O (2021) Pravovi zasady protydii movi vorozhnechi: retrospektyvnyi ohliad ta analiz perspektyv (Legal principles of counteracting hate speech). Retrospect Rev Anal Prospect 2(37):28–38

https://www.bbc.com/news/uk-england-york-north-yorkshire-51407641. Accessed 25 May 2024

Human Rights Council. Twenty-second session Agenda. Annual report of the United Nations High Commissioner for Human Rights and reports of the Office of the High Commissioner and the Secretary-General from 11 January 2013. The Office of the High Commissioner for Human Rights (UN Human Rights). https://www.ohchr.org/Documents/Issues/Opinion/SeminarRabat/Rabat_draft_outcome.pdf. Accessed 24 May 2024

Keller D (2018) Internet platforms: observations on speech, danger, and money. In: Hoover Institution's Aegis paper series no. 1807

Khavroniuk M (2022) Porushennia rivnopravnosti hromadian zalezhno vid rehionalnoi nalezhnosti: kryminalna vidpovidalnist (Violation of equality of citizens based on regional affiliation: criminal liability). https://pravo.org.ua/blogs/porushennya-rivnopravnosti-gromadyan-zalezhno-vid-regionalnoyi-nalezhnosti-kryminalna-vidpovidalnist/. Accessed 1 May 2024

Law of Ukraine on information. https://zakon.rada.gov.ua/laws/show/2657-12?find=1&text=%D0%BC%D0%BE%D0%B2%D0%B0+%D0%B2%D0%BE%D1%80%D0%BE%D0%B6%D0%BD%D0%B5%D1%87%D1%96#w2_1

Leptuga O (2019) «Mova Vorozhnechi» v ukrainomovnomu mediaprostori ("Hate speech" in the Ukrainian-language media space)

No place for hate: a Europe united against hatred. https://commission.europa.eu/news/no-place-hate-europe-united-against-hatred-2023-12-06_en. Accessed 24 May 2024

North Yorkshire Police probe racist coronavirus-related incidents. BBC. https://www.bbc.com/news/uk-england-york-north-yorkshire-51407641

Project "Without Borders" of the NGO "Social Action Center": report on the results of monitoring of hate speech in the Ukrainian media (2014). K., 78 c.

Raue B, Trier (2022) Die Regulierung von Hate Speech mit Mitteln des Zivilrechts JZ 5

Sharmar OM (2023) Osoblyvosti kryminalnoi vidpovidalnosti za porushennia rivnopravnosti hromadian zalezhno vid yikh rasovoi, natsionalnoi, rehionalnoi nalezhnosti, relihiinykh perekonan, invalidnosti, ctati ta za inshymy oznakamy v umovakh voiennoho stanu (Peculiarities of criminal liability for violation of equality of citizens based on their race, nationality, region, religious beliefs, disability, gender and other grounds under martial law). Analitychno-Porivnialne Pravoznavstvo 2:323–329

Social Media Enforcement Improvement Act (Network Enforcement Act—NetzDG). https://www.gesetze-im-internet.de/netzdg/BJNR335210017.html. Accessed 10 May 2024

The Guardian. https://www.theguardian.com/uk-news/2020/feb/09/chinese-in-uk-report-shocking-levels-of-racism-after-coronavirus-outbreak. Accessed 10 May 2024

References

The Security Service of Ukraine has served a notice of suspicion to Metropolitan Pavlo of the Ukrainian Orthodox Church (Moscow Patriarchate). https://ssu.gov.ua/novyny/sbu-povidomyla-pro-pidozru-mytropolytu-upts-mp-pavlu-video. Accessed 10 May 2024

The unified state register of court decisions of Ukraine: the verdict of the Amur-Nyzhniodniprovskyi district court of Dnipro 21 August 2023 No. case 199/6598/23. https://reyestr.court.gov.ua/Review/112928118. Accessed 10 May 2024

The unified state register of court decisions of Ukraine: the verdict of the Beregivskyi district court of the Zakarpatyya region 29 June 2023. Case No. 297/1824/23. https://reyestr.court.gov.ua/Review/111995302. Accessed 10 May 2024

The unified state register of court decisions of Ukraine: the verdict of the Kalush city district court of the Ivano-Frankivsk region 1 May 2023. Case No. 345/1885/23. https://reyestr.court.gov.ua/Review/110558242. Accessed 01 May 2024

The unified state register of court decisions of Ukraine: the verdict of the Krasnogvardiyskyi district court of Dnipropetrovsk July 2010. Case No. 204/3352/22. https://reyestr.court.gov.ua/Review/10506082. Accessed 10 May 2024

The unified state register of court decisions of Ukraine: The verdict of the Lubomlskyi district court of the Volyn region 13 June 2023. Case No. 163/1079/23. https://reyestr.court.gov.ua/Review/111543461. Accessed 01 May 20234

Wimmers/Heymann, AfP 2017, 93 (94 f.)

Xu J, Sun G, Cao W et al (2021) Stigma, discrimination, and hate crimes in Chinese-speaking world amid covid-19 pandemic. Asian J Criminol 16:51–74. https://doi.org/10.1007/s11417-020-09339-8. Accessed 1 May 2024

Chapter 6
Freedom of Speech in the Conditions of an Armed Conflict

In order to find a balance between freedom of speech and propaganda in the difficult conditions of war, one should study the judicial practice of the European Court of Human Rights regarding countries that were in military conflicts.

Freedom of speech is not an absolute right, it comes with certain duties and responsibilities. Article 10 section 2 of the ECHR establishes certain restrictions on this right to ensure national security, territorial integrity and public safety and to prevent riots or criminal offences, to protect health or morals, to protect the reputation or rights of others, to prevent the disclosure of confidential information or to maintain the authority and impartiality of the court. Restrictions cannot be established for any other purpose. Such restrictions should be necessary in a democratic society. This means that:

- there must be an urgent social need for introducing the restriction (the context, public interest, status of the person and their influence, etc. are evaluated);
- the restriction must be proportionate to the legitimate purpose (keeping a balance between the right to be protected by the restriction and the right to freedom of expression);
- the reasons for introducing restrictions must be appropriate and sufficient.

Article 15 of the Constitution of Ukraine prohibits censorship and guarantees political, economic and ideological pluralism. Article 34 of the Constitution of Ukraine guarantees everyone has the right to freedom of thought and speech, along with free expression of their views and beliefs. This right to freedom of speech means that everyone has the right to freely collect, store, use and share information. It provides a free choice of the form of obtaining information, whether orally, in writing or in another way.[1]

Mazepa (2024).

[1] Constitution of Ukraine (1996). https://zakon.rada.gov.ua/laws/show/254%D0%BA/96-%D0%B2%D1%80#Text. Accessed 10 May 2024.

The Laws of Ukraine "On printed mass media (press) in Ukraine" and "On television and radio broadcasting", which both prohibited sharing calls for the seizure of power, a violent change of the constitutional order or territorial integrity of Ukraine; propaganda of war, violence and cruelty; inciting racial, national or religious enmity; the distribution of pornography, as well as for the purpose of committing terrorist acts and other criminal acts; propaganda of communist and/or national socialist (Nazi) totalitarian regimes and their symbols; the popularisation or propaganda of the aggressor state and its authorities, representatives of those authorities and their actions, which create a positive image of the aggressor state, justify or recognise the legitimate occupation of Ukraine, etc., were revoked and replaced with the Law of Ukraine "On Media". This entered into force on 31 March 2023 as one of the seven blocks of reforms necessary for Ukraine to maintain its status as a candidate for accession to the European Union. The new rules will be introduced gradually, and the law should be fully implemented by 1 January 2031.

The Council of Europe Convention on the Prevention of Terrorism, which defines a number of measures aimed at preventing terrorism, among other things, drew attention to the danger of public provocation to commit a terrorist offence. Article 5 of this convention defines "public provocation to commit a terrorist offence" as distributing a message to the public, or bringing such a message to the attention of the public in another way, with the aim of inciting them to commit a terrorist offence, if this behaviour, regardless of whether or not it is in direct support of terrorist offences, leads to a threat that one or more such offences may be committed. Thus, the legislation of the European Union and of Ukraine contain a number of restrictions on the freedom of expression in view of the need to protect the national interests of states, ensure law and order, etc.

The armed invasion required a certain clamping down on the freedom of expression. Fierce debate erupted over when and under what conditions law enforcement agencies and courts have the right to limit freedom of expression, given the need to protect the country's national security and territorial integrity, as well as to prevent riots and crime. Government representatives, as a rule, were convinced that freedom of speech must be restricted in certain aspects in order to protect the national interests of Ukraine, while human rights defenders insisted on the need to respect all human rights, without which democracy is impossible, even in conditions of armed conflict.

These discussions demonstrated the general lack of experience in resolving such complex issues and prompted us to study the practice of the European Court of Human Rights regarding compliance with the guarantees of Article 10 of the European Convention during or in connection with an armed conflict.

6.1 Searching for a Balance Between Criticism of the Government in Wartime, a Refusal to Mobilise and the Protection of National Interests on the Example of Ukraine

Finding a balance between the right to freedom of speech and ensuring information security as a component of the state's national security is a difficult task for a state in wartime conditions. It is important to study the experience of countries that have been in similar conditions, and to study the practice of the European Court of Human Rights in cases related to restrictions on freedom of speech in armed conflict.[2]

In some cases, the European Court of Human Rights has changed its understanding of the term "development of every man" to become "each individual's self-fulfilment."[3] In this way the court has thus tried to base its freedom of expression theory[4] on both the consequentialist argument from democracy and the liberal argument from individual autonomy and self-fulfilment. In the court's jurisprudence, the argument based on democracy becomes most visible in cases involving criticism of public figures and other contributions to matters of public importance.[5]

Special attention should be paid to the case of the Ukrainian blogger and journalist Ruslan Kotsaba, against whom criminal proceedings were initiated under Article 111 section 1 and Article 114-1 section 1 of the Criminal Code of Ukraine. In 2016, Ruslan Kotsaba released a video appeal to the President of Ukraine "I am against mobilisation"[6] and called on Ukrainians to refuse to serve in the Armed Forces of Ukraine. In the video message, Kotsaba called himself a journalist of the channel "112 Ukraine". The Security Service of Ukraine accused Kotsaba of treason and opened criminal proceedings under of Article 111 Section 1 and Article 114-1 Section 1 of the Criminal Code of Ukraine (Treason and Obstructing the lawful activities of the Armed Forces of Ukraine and other military formations).

In a video message, the journalist urged people to ignore the draft and not to participate in mobilisation, citing the civil war in the east of the country.

In 2016, the court of first instance found him guilty of obstructing the Armed Forces and sentenced him to three and a half years in prison. Since the time he spent in the pre-trial detention centre was credited to him, Kotsaba had to spend a year in prison. The sentence was later overturned by appeal, but in 2017 the cassation court sent the case back for retrial.

Thus, the case ended up in the Dolyna District Court in the Ivano-Frankivsk region, which returned the indictment to the prosecutor due to lack of evidence. The

---

[2] Burmahin et al. (2019).

[3] See, for instance.

[4] Oster (2015).

[5] Oster (2021).

[6] Video appeal to the President of Ukraine "I am against mobilisation" (2016) https://www.youtube.com/watch?v=Ve_AJRn-HJA. Accessed 10 May 2024.

prosecutor's office appealed the case, and in 2019, the indictment was transferred to the Kolomyia City District Court.

Kotsaba's lawyer claimed that: "My client is recognised as a political refugee. I appealed to the Office of the United Nations High Commissioner for Human Rights, because my client was threatened with physical violence. With this organisation's help, my client has left Ukraine. He received refugee status, a passport and documents. Now the US Department of Security is taking care of his security."[7]

Ruslan Kotsaba published a video from the centre of New York, where he was walking around the city and making controversial statements about Ukraine. In particular, he talked about big problems with freedom of speech in Ukraine and that journalists can only speak positively about the current government. Then he switched to the topic of the war and began to broadcast Russian propaganda narratives that Ukraine is not a party to the conflict and that Ukrainians do not need to fight.

> He [Volodymyr Zelenskyi] is a pacifist at heart, just like me. That is, he was not going to die for the interests of the oligarchs or for the ephemeral state of Ukraine, which in fact is now getting rid of Ukrainians on its land only in the interests of the geopolitical war between the United States and Russia.

The blogger also accused Zelensky of "continuing the war, throwing thousands of new human victims into its insatiable mouth."[8]

The blogger's statements to an audience of thousands about ignoring mobilisation and denying the war can sow separatist sentiments in society and carry a potential danger to national security.

The court hearings continue to this day. This case clearly demonstrates how difficult it is to find a balance between the right to freedom of expression and the protection of national interests and the country's territorial integrity during an armed conflict. Both of these rights are reliably protected at the level of both international and national legislation.

6.2 The Issue of Ethnic Relations and Hate Speech Using the Example of Bosnia

In 1992, Bosnian Muslims and Croats voted for independence in a referendum that was boycotted by the Serbs. The European Union recognised the independence of Bosnia and Herzegovina. The war began and the Serbs defeated the capital of the country—Sarajevo—and occupied 70% of the country, killing and persecuting

---

[7] Kotsaba, accused of high treason, left Ukraine with political refugee status. (2023) https://www.unn.com.ua/uk/news/2016612-obvinuvacheniy-u-derzhavniy-zradi-kotsaba-viyikhav-z-ukrayini-zi-statusom-politichnogo-bizhentsya. Accessed 5 May 2024.

[8] Kotsaba, accused of high treason, flew to the US and recorded a video about the "ephemeral state of Ukraine" (2023). https://zn.ua/ukr/UKRAINE/obvinuvachenij-u-derzhzradi-ruslan-kotsaba-poletiv-do-ssha-i-zapisav-video-pro-efemernu-derzhavu-ukrajina.html. Accessed 5 May 2024.

6.2 The Issue of Ethnic Relations and Hate Speech Using the Example ...

Muslims and Croats. In 1995, NATO forces intervened in the conflict. A peace treaty was signed in Paris, in December 1995.

In *Smajić v Bosnia and Herzegovina* (application No. 48657/16[9]), the defendant was a lawyer who was arrested on suspicion of inciting national, racial and religious hatred, enmity or disrespect. During the case, someone claiming to be a lawyer, but using a false name, published a series of posts on a publicly accessible online forum of the website Bosnahistorija. These posts contained statements regarding a plan of action for Bosniak citizens of Brcko County in the event of war and the withdrawal of Republika Srpska (one of Bosnia's two entities and Herzegovina). The pseudonymous poster wrote:

> Bosniaks were known as Muslims before the war of 1992-1995. The term 'Bosniaks' (Bošnjaci) should not be confused with the term 'Bosnians' (Bosanci) which is commonly used to define citizens of Bosnia and Herzegovina, regardless of their ethnic origin. ...I also think that Ivići is key for Bosnians because there is a natural elevation of the terrain in the Brcko plain and from there you can see the whole city as if in the palm of your hand; having Ivići in the war is an advantage...as you can bombard the city with anything from there (I'll get some pics of the city view from be Ivići soon)...I'll do a post with pics later, I've got a lot of work to do now...it'll be stinkin' Christmas soon and it's official a holiday in Brcko, so I will have time to take a photo...if we organise things, they will have no chance of taking Brcko...The settlement of Ilicka – which has between 3,500 and 5,000 Serbs – is problematic...Ilicka and Hrcika should be hit first, as these are two key settlements. Hrcika is easy to attack because there are some Bosnians there, while Ilicka is problematic because there is no physical contact with any Bosnian settlement. In any armed scenario, we must first strike Bukvic, Gajeve and Kerik and get rid of the danger behind us, just as we did in 1992...once we deal with these Serbian villages, we will have a free corridor in the direction of Gradacak and Srebrenik. Then, in my opinion, we should attack Hrcika and Srpski Varoš...after that, the city centre should be cleared slowly, because there are many buildings there and there is a risk of heavy losses......Serbs live there who came from various shitholes; there are only a very small number of indigenous people there... Ilicka is a settlement of radical Serbs who will be the first to think of a fight with the Bosniaks from Brcko and who, in any scenario, including the exit from the Republika Srpska, should be the first to be attacked and neutralised...

The defendant did not deny that he made such statements. The main court concluded that the applicant had violated inter-ethnic relations between the "state-forming peoples" (people who declared that they were Bosniaks, Croats and Serbs) living in the Brcko district, by writing these posts on the internet, which is considered a public place within the meaning of the disputed criminal offence. The applicant and the prosecutor both filed appeals. The applicant complained that there were no elements of an offence, a "closed forum" on the internet could not be considered a "public place." He further noted that he did not incite hatred, but only expressed his personal opinion regarding a hypothetical scenario that was related to the "real world"—in particular, the frequent appeals by representatives of the highest political authorities of the Republic of Serbia to the department. In addition, the applicant noted that the case had only attracted the attention of the media after it had been publicised by the prosecutor, and only later was it written about by several daily

---

[9] *Smajić v Bosnia and Herzegovina* (application №. 48,657/16): https://hudoc.echr.coe.int/eng#{%22itemid%22:[%22001-180956%22]}. Accessed 5 May 2024.

national newspapers. The applicant further complained that his right to legal aid had been violated when he was first questioned by the police on 12 March 2010.

The Court of Appeal of the Brcko district upheld the decision of the court of first instance. The Constitutional Court of Bosnia and Herzegovina rejected the applicant's complaint as clearly unfounded. The European Court, considering the applicant's complaint, agreed that his conviction constituted an interference with the right to freedom of expression, which was provided for by the norms of criminal law and pursued one of the goals set out in in Article 10 section 2 of the Convention, namely, the protection of reputation and rights of others. The court recalled that freedom of expression is one of the basic foundations of a democratic society and one of the basic conditions for the development and the self-expression of everyone. Article 10 section 2 of the Convention applies not only to "information" or "ideas" that are positively received or considered inoffensive or to be ignored, but also to those that offend, shock or cause concern. As stated in Article 10, this freedom may be limited, but these limitations must be interpreted narrowly and their necessity must be proven beyond doubt. In addition, the court noted that it is not a "fourth instance" with respect to the decisions of national courts, but its task is to consider complaints regarding violations of the rights guaranteed by the Convention. It also recalled that, when examining the case, it must determine whether the interference was proportionate to the legitimate aim and whether the grounds given by the national authorities for its justification were appropriate and sufficient. In relation to this case, the court recalled that public authorities have more scope to assess and interpret the facts and to apply national law. At the same time, the court drew attention to the fact that the applicant had written a series of posts on a public internet forum in which he described military actions to be taken against Serbian villages and neighbourhoods in the Brcko district in the event of a war caused by Republika Srpska. According to the national courts, the publication of these posts constituted an offence as inciting national, racial and religious hatred, enmity or disrespect. The court noted that the subject of the applicant's posts, even if written in a hypothetical form, related to the very sensitive issue of ethnic relations in the post-conflict Bosnian society. In addition, the national courts carefully examined the case and, in accordance with the principles set out in Article 10 of the Convention, provided appropriate and sufficient grounds for convicting the applicant. Finally, the court noted that the nature and severity of the sanctions imposed are also factors to be taken into account when assessing the proportionality of the interference. The court emphasised that in this case the maximum sanction for the specified crime was five years in prison. The applicant was imprisoned for one year, suspended for three years, and his personal computer and laptop were confiscated. The court concluded that the sanctions imposed in this case were proportionate. Therefore, taking into account the circumstances of this case, the court considered that the interference with the applicant's right to freedom of expression did not constitute a violation of Article 10 of the Convention. Thus, the court decided that the applicant's complaint is clearly groundless and should be rejected.

6.3 The Duty of the Press to Share Information and Ideas on Policy Issues, Including Controversial Ones, and the Public's Right to Receive Them—Using the Example of Turkey

A former mayor of a Turkish city made a statement in support of the Kurdish movement (whose language had long been suppressed and the existence of a Kurdish nation was denied in 1982–1991).

On the one hand, the following statement is an encroachment on the right of freedom of speech, while on the other it is a well-founded decision by law enforcement agencies, since such a statement further inflames the conflict and is dangerous for the national security of the state. It must be remembered that, at the time when the statement of support was made, the movement was responsible for mass murders in the name of its cause. The European Court of Human Rights made a decision that the statement did not violate Article 10 of the European Convention on Human Rights.[10] The statement contained the words "I support the national liberation movement of the Kurdistan Workers' Party; on the other hand, I'm not advocating mass murder. Anyone can make mistakes and the PKK kills women and children by mistake."

Another case concerns the owner of a Turkish newspaper[11] in which articles expressing intensified hatred of the government were published, including pro-Kurdish sentiments and hate speech against the army. The European Court noted that the defendant did not associate personally with the views expressed in the articles, but it was deemed that the owner had provided the authors with a platform to incite violence and hatred. The court did not accept the applicant's argument that he should not be held criminally liable for the content of the letters, because he had a commercial, rather than a publishing relationship with the publication. The court noted that the applicant was the owner and had the authority to control the publishing direction. For these reasons, he was indirectly subject to the "duties and responsibilities" that rest on publishing houses and journalists when gathering and sharing information to society, and which become more important in situations of conflict and tension.

The court noted that there had certainly been an interference with the applicant's right to freedom of expression. It then analysed whether this was "prescribed by law", whether it pursued the legitimate aims set out in Article 10 section 2 of the Convention, and whether it was "necessary in a democratic society" to achieve those aims.

The court concluded that the interference with the applicant's right to freedom of expression was provided for by law and was aimed at protecting national security

---

[10] *Zana v. Turkey*, (application No. 69/1996/688/880), https://hudoc.echr.coe.int/tur#{%22itemid%22:[%22001-58115%22]}. Accessed 10 May 2024.

[11] *Sürek v. Turkey* (No. 1), (application No. 26682/95), https://hudoc.echr.coe.int/eng#{%22itemid%22:[%22001-58279%22]}. Accessed 10 May 2024.

and territorial integrity, as well as preventing riots and crimes (given the sensitivity of the security situation in southeastern Turkey at the time).

When considering the question of "necessity in a democratic society", the Court recalled the general principles regarding the duty of the press to share information and ideas on political issues, including those belonging to controversial ones, as well as the right of the public to receive them.[12] It was found that Article 10 had not been violated.

References

Burmahin OO, Opryshko LV, Opryshko DI (2019) Freedom of speech in the context of armed conflict. Review of the practice of the European Court of Human Rights. In: Kyiv: human rights platform NGO: 112 c

Constitution of Ukraine (1996). https://zakon.rada.gov.ua/laws/show/254%D0%BA/96-%D0%B2%D1%80#Text. Accessed 10 May 2024

Kotsaba, accused of high treason, left Ukraine with political refugee status (2023). https://www.unn.com.ua/uk/news/2016612-obvinuvacheniy-u-derzhavniy-zradi-kotsaba-viyikhav-z-ukrayini-zi-statusom-politichnogo-bizhentsya. Accessed 10 May 2024

Lindon, Otchakovsky-Laurens and July v. France (2007), applications Nos. 21279/02 and 36448/02, para. 45; *Frankowicz v. Poland* (2008), application No. 53025/99

Mazepa S (2024) A dangerous combination of propaganda and the internet in the conditions of the Russian–Ukrainian war. Law of Ukraine. No. 1

Oster J (2015) Media freedom as a fundamental right. Cambridge University Press, 30

Oster J (2021) 7. On "balancing" and "social watchdogs": the european court of human rights as a norm entrepreneur for freedom of expression". In: Callamard A, Bollinger L (eds) Regardless of frontiers: global freedom of expression in a troubled world. Columbia University Press, New York Chichester, West Sussex, 165–184. https://doi.org/10.7312/boll19698-010. Accessed 10 May 2024

Ruslan Kotsaba, accused of high treason, flew to the US and recorded a video about the "ephemeral state of Ukraine" (2023). https://zn.ua/ukr/UKRAINE/obvinuvachenij-u-derzhzradi-ruslan-kotsaba-poletiv-do-ssha-i-zapisav-video-pro-efemernu-derzhavu-ukrajina.html. Accessed 10 May 2024

Smajić v Bosnia and Herzegovina (application No. 48657/16). https://hudoc.echr.coe.int/eng#{%22itemid%22:[%22001-180956%22]}. Accessed 10 May 2024

Sürek v. Turkey (no. 1), (заява №. 26682/95). https://hudoc.echr.coe.int/eng#{%22appno%22:[%2226682/95%22],%22itemid%22:[%22001-58279%22]}. Accessed 10 May 2024

Video appeal to the President of Ukraine "I am against mobilisation" (2016). https://www.youtube.com/watch?v=Ve_AJRn-HJA. Accessed 10 May 2024

Zana v. Turkey, (application No. 69/1996/688/880). https://hudoc.echr.coe.int/tur#{%22itemid%22:[%22001-58115%22]}. Accessed 10 May 2024

---

[12] Sürek v. Turkey (no. 1), (application No. 26682/95), https://hudoc.echr.coe.int/eng#{%22appno%22:[%2226682/95%22],%22itemid%22:[%22001-58279%22]}. Accessed 18 May 2024.

Chapter 7
Conclusion

The Constitution of Ukraine allows the right to freedom of expression to be restricted on the basis of the legal interests of national security, territorial integrity or public order, in order to prevent disorder or crime, to protect public health, to protect the reputation or rights of others, to prevent the disclosure of information received in confidence, or to maintain the authority and impartiality of justice. Unlike Article 10 of the ECHR, it does not contain grounds for limiting the right to freedom of expression as necessity in a democratic society, but this issue is regulated by the fact that the norms of the European Convention on Human Rights and Fundamental Freedoms are considered part of the national legislation of Ukraine and the Law of Ukraine "On the Implementation of Decisions and Application of the Practice of the European Court of Human Rights" is in force. Article 17 of this law states that national courts, when considering cases, must apply the ECHR as a source of law.

The task of the European Court of Human Rights as a rule-maker in the field of freedom of expression is not completely fulfilled, as internet platforms and social networks require new clarifications. The ECtHR grants privileged protection to mass media, including non-governmental organisations and other "social watchdogs" (*Magyar Helsinki Bizotság v. Hungary*[1]), but the requirements for such organisations have not yet been formulated in correlation with the rules of the court on entrepreneurship, concerns the liability of internet intermediaries. Articles 12–15 of the EU's Electronic Commerce Directive set out certain immunities for internet intermediaries—access providers and hosting providers who only distribute information to third parties. However, since the EU does not is a member of the ECtHR, it cannot scrutinise the correctness of the interpretation of the e-Commerce directive, but it can only rule on whether the result of a national court's application of these provisions complies with ECHR Article 10. For example, in *Delfi v. Estonia*,[2] the

---

[1] *Magyar Helsinki Bizotság v. Hungary.* https://hudoc.echr.coe.int/fre#{%22itemid%22:[%22001-167828%22]}. Accessed 25 May 2024.

[2] *Delfi v. Estonia.* https://hudoc.echr.coe.int/fre#%7B%22itemid%22:%5B%22002-8960%22%5D%7D. Accessed 25 May 2024.

court decided that a news portal can be prosecuted for offensive comments made by readers in the comments section. The court identified the following aspects as relevant to its analysis: the context of the comments, the responsibility of the actual authors of the comments, the measures taken by the defendant company to prevent or remove the defamatory comments, and the consequences of the domestic proceedings for the applicant company. However, the Delfi Joint Opinion stated that the court "should have set out more clearly the basic principles on the basis of which it concluded that there was no violation of Article 10 [ECHR]," leaving "the relevant principles for clearer development in subsequent case law." This certainly applies to the liability not only of news portals, but also of online social networking platforms where people comment on topics that have not been raised by the service provider (such as "defamation"). Whichever path the Strasbourg Court takes, complaints about "collateral censorship" or the lack of protection of individual rights on the internet, which are contrary to the norms of antitrust law, will be inevitable.[3]

On the one hand, social media networks and the internet are important tools for protecting the right to freedom of speech and expression, which means that a person has the right to share any idea, opinion or view and receive any information. But on the other hand, international treaties and conventions prohibit propaganda of war, terrorism and discrimination, as well as propaganda of national, racial or religious hatred. In addition, a military conflict in a state can also legitimately restrict freedom of speech.

In such conditions, human rights can become human rights abuses. Our rights end where the rights of others begin, and the court seeks to balance the various rights by weighing them. There are rights that are very difficult to weigh, because it is difficult to compare them in terms of the level of intervention and the level of fundamentality.[4]

In the age of the internet, many new questions have appeared, to which the European Court of Human Rights has yet to develop principled answers. When twisted with interference with freedom of speech, it can have a chilling effect where people become afraid to speak their minds altogether, and this can lead to the destruction of the fundamental rights of democracy.

The cited case law demonstrates how difficult it is to find a balance between the right to freedom of expression and the protection of national interests and a country's territorial integrity in general, and during a period of armed conflict in particular. Both of these rights are reliably protected at the level of both international and national legislation.

Therefore, the treatment of propaganda is carried out both by treating the symptoms—introducing criminal liability for new types of propaganda and the results of the effective action of existing criminal law norms, and by preventing the development of the disease—in the form of obligations on internet platforms to detect and block propaganda, fakes and hate speech, as well as improving the international legal framework and imposing preventive measures in the form of media coverage of society and the creation of a media ecosystem. In conclusion, it is important to

---

[3] Oster (2021).

[4] Mazepa (2024).

emphasize that after the war, freedom of speech in Ukraine will be vital for national healing, and its restrictions should be reassessed. Open dialogue, even on sensitive issues, can help society process trauma, address grievances, and rebuild trust. Ensuring full freedom of expression is often essential to restoring and strengthening democratic institutions.

References

Delfi v. Estonia. https://hudoc.echr.coe.int/fre#%7B%22itemid%22:%5B%22002-8960%22%5D%7D. Accessed 25 May 2024

Magyar Helsinki Bizotság v. Hungary. https://hudoc.echr.coe.int/fre#{%22itemid%22:[%22001-167828%22]}. Accessed 25 May 2024

Mazepa S (2024) A dangerous combination of the propaganda and the internet in the conditions of the Russian–Ukrainian war. Law Ukraine 1:139

Oster J (2021) 7. On "balancing" and "social watchdogs": the European court of human rights as a norm entrepreneur for freedom of expression". In: Callamard A, Bollinger L (eds) Regardless of frontiers: global freedom of expression in a troubled world. Columbia University Press, New York Chichester, West Sussex, 165–184. https://doi.org/10.7312/boll19698-010. Accessed 25 May 2024

Printed in the USA
CPSIA information can be obtained
at www.ICGtesting.com
CBHW071557211124
17775CB00024B/455